A Path Travelled - how to make sense of relationships

# A PATH TRAVELLED

## How to Make Sense of Relationships

By Alison Blackler

To
my special friend
Caitlin

Thank you for
all you do for
everyone.

love
Alisa xx

3

First published in 2021 by 2minds publishing

Front cover design: Ross Makepeace

Typesetting and chapter illustrations: Annie Lawrenson

Photograph: Dan Dawson

ISBN 978-1-8380485-1-8

**TEAM AUTHOR UK**
*Publishing with you*

A Path Travelled - how to make sense of relationships

# DEDICATION

To Danny

The Gestalt Prayer

I do my thing and you do your thing
I am not in this world to live up to your expectations,
and you are not in this world to live up to mine.
You are you
and I am I
and if by chance we find each other,
it's beautiful.

— Fritz Perls —

## Chapter Two - New relationships

## Chapter Four -
## Challenges in relationships

**Chapter Five -**
**Leaving or ending a relationship**                  177

**" How To Make Sense Of Relationships is a beneficial book for anyone, regardless of their current relationship status. Alison guides us through life itself as much as the plethora of connections we will inevitably encounter along the way. The words and the tools within the pages are empowering for the reader whether they are happily single, unhappily married, or setting out on a journey of self love and discovery. "**

**Shelley F. Knight**

Author of Good Grief: The A to Z Approach of Modern Day Grief Healing, and Positive Changes: A Self-Kick Book.

# FOREWORD

When I was given this book to read, I must admit, being a woman of a certain age, I thought I knew all there was to know about relationships. In my younger years, I changed partners more often than my leg warmers. But then, gradually, I became tired of playing the field and ran out of leg warmers. It was time for me to settle down.

I have been married for twenty-five years and feel pretty smug about it. I mean, I must be doing something right for him to have stayed with me all this time. I know I make a mean roast dinner, but surely there's more to our relationship than that? Yes, we argue, more so in the early years, but generally, we just rub along now. I convince myself that I have trained him well.

But after reading A Path Travelled - how to make sense of relationships, I have to admit to having my eyes opened. I have started to appreciate the complexities of my marriage, how our behaviours affect each other, and how we have evolved. While the book is aimed at couples, it throws a spotlight on your own habits. Sometimes the spotlight is harsh, and it was these sections of the book I found particularly fascinating.

Alison Blackler explores and translates how past relationships, including those you witnessed and experienced as a child, alter and affect your behaviour, reactions and communications. Her analysis of why we react differently to situations or environments I found particularly intriguing. I now find that I shouldn't presume I am right simply because I can shout louder than him. I now examine my partner's reason for not agreeing and realise that it is not always because he can't be bothered, listen, or simply because he's a man! (But sometimes it is.)

The book examines a wide range of relationships, including the bad ones. My past is littered with men of questionable taste, bad manners and noisy eaters, and we've all been with the partner that totally disrespected us. I always looked at these with an element of regret, but after reading this book, Alison offers an alternative way of processing those memories and feelings and how to apply them in a positive way today.

With exercises for you to complete, this book offers a safe space for you to cogitate and express yourself. It encourages honesty and deep reflection while making you still feel normal. We all know we can be a crank, but it was comforting to know that a lot of people are cranks too. We are all human and we all want to be loved.

*A Path Travelled – how to make sense of relationships* is not a book that tells you how to make a relationship work. It simply offers the reasons why some do, some don't, and some are not supposed to. Alison has produced a wonderfully insightful book that felt very personal to me, proving what an excellent writer she is. I will no doubt return to this time and time again, especially when he gets on my nerves!

*Estelle Maher – Author, Blogger*

# Let Us Begin

# Trusting the journey of life

My professional and personal journeys have always ran parallel. I am a mind coach. This means that I have studied human behaviours through a range of qualifications including a coach, counsellor, CBT therapist and I have studied neuro-linguistic programming. This all runs along with my own experiences and an interest I developed in looking at my own patterns, beliefs and habits. Even though we often learn about ourselves through challenging and difficult experiences, being able to see and trust that good will come is critical.

Just like most of us, the journey I have been on has been interesting, with both highs and lows. Each stage has got me nearer and nearer to being the 'real' me. Over time, being able to see what was behind some of the decisions, limits and uncertainty, gave me answers so that I could make changes.

When you come from a place of knowing that there will be answers and a different approach to challenges, then that curiosity becomes the vehicle.

My own relationship experiences have given me insights, empathy and a truth I want to share with you in this book.

## This book

Following the success of *A Path Travelled – How to make sense of your life*, this book is specifically focused on intimate relationships.

*A Path Travelled – How to make sense of your life*, my first published book, is mainly focused on working on yourself, so that you know who you are, explore what holds you back and can navigate yourself on your own true path. We explored the functions of the mind, how childhood and past experiences impact our adult lives and looked at tools to help you create self-belief and increase confidence.

Most aspects of life are linked to a relationship of some sorts - one with yourself, your family, friends, colleagues and obviously intimate ones, therefore there were areas to explore in more depth, hence this book.

This book is as much focused on each person in the relationship as the relationship itself. It is healthier to see a relationship as two individuals coming together in unison rather than just two people becoming one. While the latter might sound romantic, it can leave you feeling unfulfilled, stifled and miserable.

This book is also designed to help all relationships regardless of sexuality. As each relationship can be slightly different for any couple, there will be similarities as two people come together.

There will be elements from A Path Travelled – How to make sense of your life throughout this book when relevant. The functions of the mind and how we behave are complex to understand, so hearing them many times over is always a good thing. It will enhance your growth and development and is key to intimate relationships.

This book can be read through quickly, going back over the exercises in your own time or read by section to then relate it to yourself. This approach means that you take your time to reflect and understand. Throughout the book, there are exercises and case studies to support the content, encouraging you to explore your own relationships and life.

Keep in mind, it is one thing knowing the theory and another utilising it and putting it into practice. Be patient and kind to yourself on this journey.

The aim of this book is for you to be fast-tracked in your understanding of yourself, yourself in relationships and then understanding intimate relationships. It will help you look at your relationship, your relationship patterns and habits and most importantly, understand the part you play. All the way through, the content could be relating to your behaviours, or the behaviours of another whom you are affected by. Keep in mind: is it referring to you and is it you that needs to change? Or could it be another who is creating the behaviour?

This book could be read by a couple together to help them make sense of their relationship. This is a clearly positive step and could reduce drama or conflict by working together. A word of warning, this may not be the right approach for all couples.

There is a need for consideration between improving a relationship and acknowledging that it is over. This book will outline many factors to help you consider which is the right path for you. Sometimes you need to recover from old wounds first so that you can be successful in a relationship. This can be done within a relationship and may take much patience. Sometimes things do not work out because the match was wrong, or maybe you deserved better. We will be exploring what is often at the root of such situations.

Later in this book, we will focus on good communication, mindful interpretation and appreciation of others. We will explore what unhealthy relationships look like, why we stay in them and the challenging issue of leaving one. We will look at how to attract the right kind of person and how you can maintain a healthy relationship so that each of you flourishes.

## Setting the scene

Relationships are complex and probably one of our biggest challenges. Most adults spend much of their life in an intimate relationship. The fact that you have picked this book up probably means that you are either in a relationship and would like to improve it, need to heal from one, or would like to be in one.

" Relationships take one form or another ... "

Relationships are potentially satisfying. They protect us from loneliness and can improve our mental and emotional wellbeing. However, they can be challenging, and many different issues can cause couples disturbances. There are obviously arguments, fights and power struggles, but there are also stress-related reactions to each other, leading to further problems.

Challenges can build up in a relationship over a period of time, increase in frequency or create difficult consequences. The job is to work out what is acceptable and what is not. Each person's relationship is unique, just like the people in them. Couples can experience turbulent phases, which can lead to much needed changes, or the relationship may become too difficult to continue. Relationships can feel stressful, and our aim here is to consider the wider perspective. Some of the examples, particularly in the unhealthy relationship chapter, may seem extreme. However, keep in mind that any behaviour can happen with a varying degree of discomfort, and it is for each couple to decide what is acceptable.

For some, it can look like a relationship is easy and natural, although there is usually work and commitment aplenty. When relationships work well, there is give and take, respect, honesty and positive regard. With the right balance of compromise and flexibility, it is vital to allow each person to flourish within the relationship. This all sounds so idealistic, and the reality of life and, indeed, relationships, make this an interesting journey.

Life is full of experiences, some of which work well and some not so much. As explored in *A Path Travelled – How to make sense of your life*, challenges can be useful to help us grow and develop.

If everything were plain sailing, our personal journey would probably be limited. While we clearly need some time of stability, we learn the most from challenging situations. The trick is to see these as a chance to change rather than as a negative experience. Relationships take work and commitment, though focusing on yourself first is critical. This understanding gives peace and clarity.

Almost all couples will have misunderstandings, conflicts and disagreements. We will each do things that annoy the other. It is fair to say, 'all relationships take work'. However, we must not get confused with those that leave us exhausted and drained. It should not constantly feel like hard work. There must be a balance and knowing this balance can make all the difference.

Being in the wrong relationship is no one's fault; it can be an honest mistake. When it is a real challenge is when you and a partner are essentially mismatched. There is no way to change or reconcile — the best thing to do is to recognise it for what it is and get out as compassionately as possible.

Some of the challenges and issues explored in this book may occur within any relationship. There is no judgement as the complexity of a relationship can mean that it will hit challenges. The idea is to look at things from a different perspective to see if there is any need for change, whether that be yourself or both.

## Ourselves

It is right to say that the biggest challenge we face is the relationship we have with ourselves. This then influences any relationship with another person, particularly an intimate one. We are often focused externally and see problems with these relationships, rather than looking internally at ourselves.

" The biggest challenge we face is the relationship with ourselves.... "

When you have a difficult time with your own thoughts, beliefs, and behaviours, relationships with others will be equally challenging. This can be where the root cause lies.

Most relationships can become like a habit. It is natural and inevitable that the two people become relaxed and settled with each other further into the relationship. While this is great for relationships that have enough good habits, it is very damaging when the bad behaviours have become the norm.

As humans, we have an innate desire to be liked, loved, fit in, and are not keen on upsetting another person. Our behaviours are often driven by this need, which does not always end well.

It is vital to be able to understand yourself first before you can try to decipher how someone else is thinking or behaving. It is key to remember that everyone is not thinking and feeling the same as you. Knowing this helps you to adjust your expectations and improve relationships with others. When it starts to go wrong, we rely on our own interpretation of a situation and use this to put meaning onto another.

The key to a healthy relationship, especially an intimate one, is to notice your own behaviours, be brave and admit your flaws. Sometimes these are only obvious through viewing your behaviour alongside someone else. As you get to know them, you often learn more about yourself through their different ways of being. When you are aware enough to realise this, it pushes you to change, even though at the time it may feel awful.

## We are all unique

Our uniqueness comes from so many different factors, so there is no wonder that we are often on a different page from one another. Through our upbringing, our experiences, our past, we all have our own story to tell, although the way all these experiences are processed makes it even more complex. This interpretation can get in the way when we are communicating with others and we will be exploring the many ways that affects our relationships.

As incredible as we are, we have many challenges which are not necessarily echoed in the animal kingdom. We are limited in our ability to truly understand others: why others do the things they do, why others say the things they say and what they actually mean. Some situations, and even conversations, can feel like a mystery. This is because we all process and interpret everything differently. Each person can interpret the same situation in another way even though on the surface, it will look the same. The description of the situation can appear similar; same place, same time, same day, although a different interpretation. There are traits that look, sound or feel the same, although the actual experience is unique.

Take a moment to read this case study, which demonstrates this point so simply.

A couple walking down the road spot their neighbour walking towards them. The woman says to her husband, "Oh look, there's Peter from next door." She raises her arm to wave. At that instant, Peter steps closer to the curb, checks for oncoming cars and makes his way to the other side of the street.

Her arm is left hanging in a half wave and the smile falls from her face.

She turns to her husband and says, "What have we done wrong? I bet he is irritated because we left our bins out overnight last Thursday. He's not speaking to us."

Her husband replies, "Don't be silly. He's in a hurry and didn't even see us." She is in a place of low self-esteem, ready to blame herself for the neighbour's actions and could easily cause an issue within the relationship.

Her husband is more likely in a place of high self-esteem, seeing the same scenario as an innocent occurrence, no one to blame, nothing unusual, his day and his relationship with Peter unaffected.

## Interpretations

The human mind is wired to experience the world as we believe it to be. This means that our minds process and store information from a situation and then uses this information to make sense of the present moment. Remembering this helps us to understand why we all interpret differently and where conflict can often lie.

The mind is an association-making machine. This means that in any situation, each person will retrieve their associated information stored within their mind in an attempt to make sense of the current situation. Sometimes this associated information is unhelpful and even irrelevant. This explains how the same situation can and will be interpreted differently. Each person's memory and interpretation of the situation is 100% right for them, but the problem lies in the fact that each person thinks the same! This is often at the root of most disagreements.

With this in mind, we assume that the other person has experienced the same as us. Most people think that we see to believe, but we actually believe to see. The mind has altered the memory of the images to be as we believe them to be, and we then believe that this is what we originally saw. Our minds do the believing, not our eyes. When we each have this happening, this can lead to the chance of a different interpretation.

## Communication

All communication has two parts: a sender and a receiver. The sender has a message he or she intends to transmit, and this is put into words or actions which is believed to best reflect what is in their mind. But many things can intervene to prevent the intended message from being received correctly.

Given our tendency to hear what we expect to hear, it is easy for people in conflict to misunderstand each other. Communication is strained, and people will, most likely, want to hide the truth to some extent. The potential for misperceptions and misunderstandings is high, which can make a resolution more difficult.

With this understanding, we can start to see a different and complex perspective of why communication is such a challenge at times. What we have not mentioned yet is that the part of the mind which interprets information first is the emotional part. It is said this emotional response is five times quicker than anything rational. Immediate responses are often unwarranted or inappropriate. So, when our initial response to everything, literally everything, is an emotional one, and each person has their own model of the world, it makes for an interesting dilemma.

Social media needs a 'shout out' here. It has changed the way we communicate, and it does leave us open to more challenges. The risks of miscommunication and wrong interpretation have increased so much. There are also the issues associated with being able to track someone, see where they are, who they are with and sometimes this information can blow-up situations unnecessarily.

## Family experiences

There are many influences throughout our childhood, including society, family dynamics and our environment. There is the big debate of nature versus nurture. Some think that your personality is based on genetic predispositions, nature, pre-wiring influenced by genes and other biological factors.

Others conclude that nurture is the predominant factor - the way we act stems from the influences of external factors, life experience, the way we were taught, and the environment in which we grew up.

The nature versus nurture debate will go on and on. Whichever you believe, it is accurate to say our upbringing has a big impact on how we are moulded.

Initially, we are affected by the people who cared for us, as well as other family members. Then we become influenced by our friends, our friends' parents, our siblings' friends, work colleagues, intimate relationships and adult friendships. All these relationships shape us throughout the years, and, of course, we ourselves are influencers in other people's lives.

Difficulties in adult relationships can stem from a lack of emotional and psychological support as a child. For example, in the way love and affection were shown. This is vital when we are forming our identity. However, when this support is missing, it often results in someone not knowing who they are and lack belief in themselves. When any of our emotional needs are not met, the outcome is that we unconsciously feel unworthy.

It is common that we behave as we have been shown. We will often behave in relationships as we observed in our parents' behaviour. This is not a pre-requisite, and we can choose to be the complete opposite. It comes down to how aware we are of our behaviour. Some people in a relationship give in the same loving way they were brought up; some who were over-protected may become over-protective partners. If someone was shouted at or even hit, there is a chance they will copy this behaviour, although not a given. When criticism is the primary mode of communication, they are likely to be like this in a relationship. Our parents are our first role models, and in fact, our first managers too! Everything, and we mean everything, influences us and is part of how we are shaped and moulded as adults.

This can also play out in who we are attracted to. It is often said that we meet someone like our own parents. For example, a young man growing up with an overbearing mother may be attracted to other overbearing women not because he likes being dominated but rather because it is what he considers normal.

## Differences

As we are all unique, this means we are naturally going to have differences in many ways. Having differences in a relationship is normal and healthy. Differences of opinion and interests can enrich a relationship. We can be introduced to new and different things, and this can enhance your life. It might be new hobbies, new foods, or other experiences. However, these can also be at the root of challenges within relationships.

In a healthy relationship, the trick is to work with each other's differences instead of seeing them as ⌐hallenge. Relationships can become stronger if ⌐an talk about differences and use them to enhance the relationship. It is also vital to be able to talk about stresses and strains and have this as a normal part of the relationship. Conflict can often be resolved, and serious matters dealt with through respectful communication and a bit of give and take.

Being somewhat different from your partner can make your relationship more fun and exciting. Both partners need to be willing to adjust, flex, or maybe give things up for the sake of a better relationship. The process of negotiation will only make the relationship stronger, as well as each person.

Successful couples can have differences intellectually, socially, morally, politically, economically and culturally. These are often easier to understand and agree on. It is understanding different interpretations that can have the greatest impact.

A clash of differences may often be the first problem encountered. For example, one partner wanting to spend money freely while the other wants to save. They may have friends who do not get along with their partner or may have different educational backgrounds. All these will weaken the heady feeling of being in love and expecting to remain 'happy ever after'.

There is a need for interpersonal skills to understand and resolve the differences. Tolerance, patience, understanding and negotiating skills are all important, although these are easier said than done if other behaviours and thinking are not paid attention to first.

## Someone 'like' us

The more 'like' someone we are, the nearer a good experience there will be. When we feel like we just click with someone, there is a probability that some of their internal, unconscious processing is the same as ours. There are the obvious common interests that bind people together, although the real connections come from something much deeper.

It is not surprising that we tend to like people who are like us, though the reasons why we like people who are like us can be complex. Firstly, there is a difference between having a lot in common with someone and then believing that we have a lot in common. These two kinds of similarity are certainly related but are not the same thing.

These scenarios play out when we meet anyone, whether it be a friendship or an intimate relationship. You may initially think you have a lot in common with someone but find out later that you were mistaken. Or you might assume you will have a lot in common with a person because you have some shared interests or experiences, only to find out that you are not really on the same wavelength once you get to know each other. Or another scenario is that you may assume you have a lot in common with someone just because you like them. There are also many different reasons why we might like people who are like us. Perhaps we anticipate that someone who has a lot in common with us will like us more. Or maybe we just find it more fun to hang out with someone who shares our interests.

## People come into your life for a reason

This book will help you to explore and understand why some people have come into your life. It is too common to hear that failed relationships are only ever seen as a bad thing rather than an opportunity to grow. When relationships are defined as bad only, it is very likely to affect self-confidence, beliefs and the future. We stay damaged because we are not able to understand what happened, what part we played and what we can take positively into the future.

It helps us to understand that people respond differently in situations. When we learn to step back, notice what and why things are happening, we gain valuable feedback. Taking a step back allows a complete change in perception of these situations and is like a fresh pair of eyes. These can become little 'gems' of feedback, lessons in life, relationships and love, and it is these that will bring us closer to our own path and happiness.

A simple explanation is that people come into your life for a reason. We often meet people at the perfect time. Some people can meet a partner and it was perfect timing, the right person and we could say, 'they lived happily ever after'. This is obviously an ideal and hopefully happens to everyone eventually. They say that the right 'one' is out there for each of us, and this book will help us to understand why this often takes longer for some.

" People come in to your life for a reason... "

When you reflect on past relationships through a new lens, you can start to see why some people did come into your life and how they helped you. This reflection will provide valuable and powerful insights to grow from.

Being able to see all past relationships as a reason rather than a failure is a better position than feeling heartbroken, damaged or filled with regret. When you see these relationships, which may have been very challenging, as a gift to you, then you can move forward.

A word of warning, though, you must take the learning; otherwise, you will find yourself in the resit class. The resit class is being in a similar position again and again because you have not been able to see what the situation is showing you. Hence, people come into your life for a reason.

## Self-limiting beliefs

It is important for us to explore self-limiting beliefs here. It is vital to understand how each partner's limiting self-beliefs will affect the relationship.

When we have conflict with ourselves, it is often a challenge between our conscious desire and our subconscious mind trying to protect us. This can manifest as something we will call self-sabotage, a true battle of the minds! Self-sabotage refers to behaviours and thought patterns that hold a person back and prevent them from doing what they want. An example is procrastination, imposter syndrome or comfort eating.

We all seem to self-sabotage at times, some more than others. This is where we get in the way of ourselves and limit our potential. In situations that our minds have interpreted as 'dangerous', we will get a fight, flight or freeze response which is normal. The mind's primary job is to protect us, although this protection is often being triggered unnecessarily.

All experiences create a memory within, and from here, we can construct a set of beliefs about ourselves. As with anything in life, some of these are clearly good and help us, while others are negative and limiting.

It is all too common that many of us have created a belief that we are not good enough. This defines us and drives many of our decisions. It can play out in a very obvious way, but more often subtly and is often seen in how we behave in intimate relationships.

As humans, we judge ourselves against others, limit our achievements and generally create doubts. We will interpret situations against ourselves and then 'make up' another's response. We can find ourselves thinking that people do not like us, or we have upset them.

An example of this may be when someone does not reply to a message. You automatically interpret that they are ignoring you on purpose and that you must have done something wrong. While this clearly could be true, it is more often the case that we have mixed our own feelings with what we think we are experiencing.

We so often misinterpret other's actions. This processing all happens in a blink of an eye and you are left with an emotional response related to your thoughts. You may feel upset, angry, or even devastated. By starting to understand this whole cycle, we can see issues differently and get an idea of what holds us back.

For any of us, limiting beliefs can be created at any time in life. Some do come from childhood and old past experiences, although they can be created and reinforced in current situations. You may have believed in yourself, but a difficult relationship has knocked your confidence. The trick is to notice them, their impact and address them before real problems start.

These beliefs will continue to be reinforced by our own thinking, often regardless of the external world. Remember, we said the mind is an association-making machine. Whatever you believe about yourself, the subconscious mind will look for evidence and reinforcement in the current situation. We tell ourselves a story, and the mind continues to make this as truth.

Our internal negative thinking, behaviours and how we respond to them, are all indicators that the limiting beliefs are running the show. It is all too common to spend days, weeks, months and even years in some cases, chewing over the same kind of thinking. This is often related to someone or something that has happened, particularly when we believe we were hurt, let down or wronged. Dwelling on the past becomes a pastime. The energy and emotion that this takes up is draining and can harm us physically, mentally and emotionally. This has a direct impact on confidence, trust and happiness.

## Comparing to others

It is a human trait to compare ourselves to others. This can be a positive experience if we are using it as a motivator. We can use others as a catalyst for making positive changes. What is unhealthy is when we compare ourselves negatively. This becomes an unhealthy experience because we are not comparing like for like. We never know what is happening 'behind closed doors', and therefore, we can be comparing on a false idea. It will often result in any self-limiting thoughts to be at large.

When we feel 'less' than someone else, this will affect any relationship. When there is a perceived imbalance, this is likely to have a negative impact and is usually feeding limiting self-beliefs.

We are social animals, and we gain a sense of self by observing others. The lives of others can provide perspective and, sometimes, reassurance. We process the information people share about themselves and, consciously or not, log that against our personal experience. We do not live in an autonomous bubble, so who else but other people can be our barometer of normality?

How would we know what was acceptable, awful, brilliant, or routine unless it was by comparisons with others? And no area of our lives is more susceptible

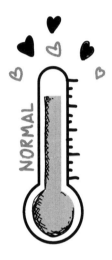

for anxious comparisons than our romantic relationships.

When we constantly compare ourselves to others unfavourably, we waste precious energy focusing on other peoples' lives rather than our own. Comparisons often result in sadness and even resentment towards others and ourselves. Negative comparison can deprive us of joy.

Have you ever been in company with another couple who seem loved-up and close?

Have you found yourself asking why your partner is not like that with you?

We can think that someone is happier than us and become so focused on it that it stops us from being ok in our own relationship. We can also stop ourselves from moving forward because we are too busy thinking that everyone else's life is better than ours and then not taking action for ourselves.

## What will others think?

Another area to be aware of is the common habit of being concerned by what others think of us. In fact, we are governed by what others expect of us. This can be another reason why we get on the wrong life track. These situations can lead to feeling insecure, stifled, trapped, confused and often lonely because we are not following our own path.

Worrying too much about what other people think of you is very likely to hold you back. Frequently, people indulge their need to be liked so much so that it dictates the way they behave. We then make decisions within or about our relationship because of what others think, or even what we believe others are saying.

It is common for relationships to be struggling because there is too much influence from outside, sometimes family or often, the wider society. There can be pressure within the relationship from any type of comparison to others. This is a strong reminder that finding the right path for you and your relationship is vital to happiness.

It is ironic that in so many areas of our lives, we strive for individuality. We want to separate ourselves from homogeny with our personalities, our opinions, and our style. Yet, when it comes to relationships, we aspire towards 'normality', to be like everybody else, because it gives us a glimpse at a map that is completely unknowable. When you are with a friend and have the 'OMG, me too!' moment during an open conversation, you realise that you both understand each other.

## Social and true self

It is worth mentioning here that we are often challenged in our decisions between our social self and our true self. Some people will feel complete when they are in a relationship because society says this is the right path. This need is driven by the social self. It is the 'norm' to be in a relationship and therefore 'abnormal' not to be in one. This, of course, is just an idea, although a very powerful driver for many. The need to conform and be a couple can drive someone to start a relationship with 'anyone', and certainly not necessarily a suitable person.

This situation of making decisions based on what others and society say is right, is a risk. We make the wrong choices because we are not allowing our true self to lead the way.

We are often driven by society's expectations of us, and this is shaped by what we imagine others think or expect. For example, you might find yourself wanting to get married because that is what is expected of you and yet this may not be what you truly want.

What can be right for one person is certainly not right for all. It can feel like we 'should' be doing what is expected. We can feel bombarded by so many different influencers telling us what is acceptable in our life, including our families, friends, the media, and the wider society in general.

A relationship is the normal path for many people, although ensuring that it is the right relationship for each individual is key.

A question that has a range of answers is: 'Is it better to be single than be with the wrong person?' The answer often lies with the driver for being in a relationship and whether it is negative. When feeling the need to be with someone to complete you or just to fit in, you are heading for a crash.

Because of the impact of other people's opinions and an innate desire to fit in and not upset anyone, we often ignore our own needs and hopes.

## Being honest with yourself

In the spirit of being honest with yourself, it is time now to start to truly see your part in previous or current relationships. This is likely to be a game changer.

Think back to a situation or situations when you felt hurt; your emotions were uncontrollable. Do you dwell on this situation or constantly let the other person know about your hurt? As we have said, in these situations, we are so often externally focused, and it is time to look at ourselves. These behaviours need to be reined in, as they are exhausting for everyone and can destroy the relationship.

The truth is your behaviours are more likely to be driven by your own thinking and could be triggering insecurities and doubt. This response could be a message that you should be doing something differently.

If you notice and change your thoughts, the shift in focus will make a difference. When you start to take responsibility, you can decide what you would like to happen. Wouldn't it be better to be able to settle and soothe yourself when someone changes a plan or does not act as you had expected, rather than heading for a meltdown?

Also, it is much better to move away from thinking that someone else is ruining or taking over your life, and to notice that someone else has way too much control. Just to clarify again, we are not saying that we must accept other people's poor behaviour. For example, if someone is constantly cancelling or changing arrangements, then we can feel upset or annoyed initially. If someone is being moody and uncooperative, you are not expected to accept this.

However, when we start to take control, put a different kind of attention on scenarios when your automatic response is highly emotional, self-deprecating, or you assume it is because of you, then you will notice a difference.

## How we see ourselves

What we see in the mirror can be different from what others perceive when they look at us.

When you look at yourself in a mirror, what you see depends on the quality of that mirror. The mirror being your version of mostly your internal thoughts, feelings and beliefs. It is also connected to how you perceive any external forces, such as how you think others see you. Our self-image makes a huge difference in how we feel and act.

To get you started, this next exercise is an opportunity to do a little self reflective. Complete this next exercise carefully and respectfully towards yourself.

# STEP to CHANGE

## A True Perspective

# A True Perspective

Take some time to think about your own situation. It is important to be honest and non-judgemental.

1)      What am I afraid to know?

2)      What is the one thing I least want to accept?

3)     What do I sense without knowing?

4)  What do I make up about myself?

## Blind spots

We all have our way of seeing ourselves, and it's often not favourable. We also have some behaviours that are out of our awareness and therefore within a 'blind spot'. This means that they are unconscious to us and can be seen by others. An emotional blind spot is like the human eye.

Some behaviours are innocent, like a 'quirk' and do not cause us much difficulty. They do not need to be pointed out and are not offensive. Sometimes these can be seen as annoying habits, and someone might feel the need to point it out. This, at worst, can be interpreted as criticism.

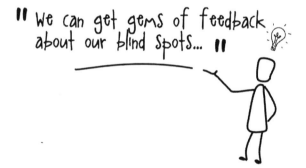

Our blind spots can be present in our auto-responses, our behaviours, our thinking patterns and in our language. We are unable to see them unless we become curious, ask questions and consider feedback from others. These approaches will help us to grow and make changes. Sometimes we ignore feelings and block experiences because they are unpleasant or confusing. This can be because something is happening in our blind spot. An example of this might be feeling unsettled when someone is overriding our hopes or needs, and it could be that we need to acknowledge our own lack of assertiveness. It's this lack of assertiveness that is our blind spot.

We can also be blind to information that is troubling, frightening, or opposed to what we believe and, to absorb it, would shatter our view of ourselves and the world. The tracks that a blind spot leaves are repetitive experiences that seem inexplicable, the things that make you exclaim, 'Why does this always happen to me?'. We will be looking at this later in the book when we explore the resit class.

An example is you keep having the same kind of relationship or meeting a similar type of partner. Out of your awareness is the fact that you are choosing partners who match certain profiles, or that their behaviours elicit similar reactions from almost everyone you encounter. Hence, 'Why does this keep happening to me?'.

Another pattern in behaviours is when you think, 'My luck never changes'. Those who complain of relentless bad luck in relationships are likely to continue on this path. A choice is far more powerful than chance in determining the pattern of your failures and successes over time. When someone does well in a relationship, they have probably found ways to learn from their experiences and have a great ability to bounce back should they need.

A blind spot may be evident when someone consistently describes you in a way that does not fit with your own self-image.

If tracking patterns in love and luck is not enough to reveal your blind spots, there is another way to go after them. You can take time to notice what people tell you about yourself — the things you have always cleverly ignored or routinely discounted.

We will be coming back to blind spots later as they are such a critical part of our behaviours.

Complete the exercise as accurately as you can. You might be closing in on a truth you have not fully acknowledged.

# STEP to CHANGE

## Your Blind Spots

## Your Blind Spots

Take some time to complete these sentences:

"People are always telling me that I'm..."

"I get a lot of compliments about..."

"When my friends or family members are angry with me, they say that…"

"People often thank me for…"

If any of the descriptions from the previous exercise seem strange, incongruous, or flat-out false, consider the possibility that your image of yourself may not be accurate and almost certainly does not correspond to what other people perceive. You may well discover that you are blind to your positive characteristics as well as negative ones.

In this chapter, we have explored the many aspects of ourselves which have an impact on who we are and therefore our relationships.

In the next chapter, we will be exploring new relationships including the joys and challenges of those. We will start with this as it is good to understand what is happening right at the beginning of a relationship.

This chapter is worth a read even if you are not looking for, or are not in, a new relationship as you will no doubt gain some insights for yourself.

# CHAPTER TWO

# New Relationships

To begin our exploration of relationships, it is important to put some attention onto new relationships, what they are like and how we can ensure that they are worth pursuing.

In this chapter, we will look at some of the chemistry behind a new relationship and how to navigate this to ensure a healthy relationship is the end result.

When we were younger, we naively assumed that when we found the ideal person, it would be easy, and we were going to feel comfortable and safe all the time. We would float on clouds, feeling blissful and light, and that we would love everything that person did. That surely is what being with 'The One' would feel like. Of course, most of us have these feelings right at the beginning of a new relationship. It is, however, good to understand this a little more as there are traps and challenges to be mindful of.

## Love addiction

There is literally nothing nicer than the feelings we get when we first meet someone we like. If it could be bottled, I think we would all buy it.

In new relationships, there is an urgency to see each other and be together. We can almost feel like we are 'losing the plot' as different hormones are released into the body. At the beginning, we can get confused about the feelings we have and can fall into the trap of thinking that it is true love.

How can we say that we love someone we have just met?

We may daydream about what it might be like, how the relationship might develop and all the romantic things we hope for. This is all very normal with no issue, except when we hold firmly onto the idea of the person or what the relationship might be. We can then be blind to other issues yet to unfold, as we are focused on the dream we want.

Being in love is a calculated risk – we are putting our hearts in someone else's hands, and that element of uncertainty inevitably fosters insecurity. It is only natural that we seek reassurance through the relationship.

In the early days of dating, it is typical to want to invest and feel 'head-over-heels' in love. Coupled with the chemical response, we have each person in the relationship's different model of the reality, which includes each person's interpretation and expectations of the relationship.

## Stages of love

The first stage in most new relationships is bliss! You are perfect, the other person is perfect, and the relationship just flows. You make time for one another whenever you can, you communicate with each other constantly, and it just feels easy.

There are no triggers or things the other person does to upset you; the attraction is 'unreal', and you think, 'This is it! I have finally found the one! Finally, I can rest'.

It is easy to play down things we do not like or make us uncomfortable because we are in this blissful place. We are on 'our best behaviour' and would not want to complain about anything.

When we fall in love, we develop irrational beliefs and desires. There is a risk that we allow our lives to be consumed by the person with whom we are infatuated. This feels great — it is intoxicating.

The problem with allowing your identity to be consumed by a romantic relationship is that as you change to be closer to the person you love, you cease to be the person they fell in love with in the first place.

## Falling 'in love' chemical

Let us look at a little science behind when we meet someone new. It is good to remember the impact when our bodies are flooded with the feel-good chemical, Oxytocin. This triggers specific physical reactions and is the falling in love chemical. It is the same chemical that is naturally produced when a woman breastfeeds a baby.

People often say, 'I feel like I am sixteen again'. We are driven by the sex hormones testosterone and oestrogen, and research shows that early love, the attraction phase, really changes the way we think.

There is a physical reaction, never mind what it does to our thinking and behaviours. For some, you cannot eat, cannot get them out of your head, cannot wait to see them again and feel like you cannot live without them — all very normal and joyful. The Oxytocin affects our brain to an extent where we cannot think straight - 'giddy in love'. When we can recognise that going through this 'youth-like' feeling is something that we have to go through, we can simply enjoy it.

## Rose-tinted glasses

With these chemicals flying around, we need to be mindful that these affect our judgement and decision making. Initially, we may worry about what we say or how we behave because we want the other person to like us. This desire to be liked is a human trait. However, it can get us into trouble. Too often, people make quick promises and even plans during this time which are certainly not guaranteed to be right.

During this time, the goal is to simply enjoy a flighty, fun, romantic time, often referred to as the 'honeymoon period' and resist anything else. The mind will let you believe that nothing could possibly go wrong and we probably all know a time when we have been completely caught out.

"In the honeymoon period, we are on our best behaviour..."

In the 'honeymoon period', we are likely to be on our 'best behaviours', being very flexible and amenable and ignoring flaws in the other one, hence the 'rose-tinted glasses'. We might have spotted something in ourselves or our partner which does not feel right, but we hope it will go away. The reality is that each one is not really showing their true self, so each is in the same boat.

We know that there are many other factors involved here, such as one liking the other more or one being more ready for a relationship than the other. But for now, we just need to know that there is a high chance that the real person has not turned up to the relationship yet, despite it feeling amazing.

## Jumping in

These hormones act like a shield for anything that is not quite right, and a couple often end up 'jumping in' without knowing what they are jumping into. There are so many promises, plans and hopes made between the couple, and some just in our own minds. These often are not part of the reality. It is tempting and natural to want to talk about the future when everything feels right, but the issue here is you do not actually know it is right – yet!

In these early days, it is likely that you will feel like, 'I have met the one'. Your mind is running away with you. This time is simply better to be enjoyed for what it is rather than getting too carried away. Easier said than done.

As time passes, the chemicals start to settle down and then the real relationship can start. Or, in some cases, the real challenge begins.

After a short while, you both start to relax and settle into being 'yourself'. Some barriers are let down and some truths start to come out. While this is all normal, this is still a time to be mindful and aware. The real people need to establish if there is a true connection.

It is vital that we can be ourselves in a relationship, and so often, this is not the case. Later in the book we will look many unhealthy behaviours within a relationship when this happens, although this is important to mention it . A new relationship can come with a warning sign and time will reveal the truth. We have our own gut instinct to tell us if things are ok, although this is often switched off or ignored in these early stages.

Quite often, in a new relationship, the desire for it to work out overtakes the need to be honest and pay attention to little signs that let you know if it is going in the right direction.

It needs stating here that many people are fortunate enough to meet someone and for the relationship to be successful. We are saying that we need to be mindful that jumping in too early and not paying attention to differences and possible challenges, even within ourselves, is vital in the initial 'love addiction' phase.

In this phase, it is common to either ignore challenges or start to change yourself so much that you become miserable. We will look at challenging behaviours later on, but it is important to highlight the loop as it can start right at the beginning.

## The fear kicks in

It is not until further into the relationship, the attachment phase, that we can truly know that we have fallen in love.

During this phase, a couple are setting a foundation for the relationship and building a connection. By now, the 'love addiction' phase has passed. The relationship is changing, the connection grows deeper and stronger, and this is completely natural.

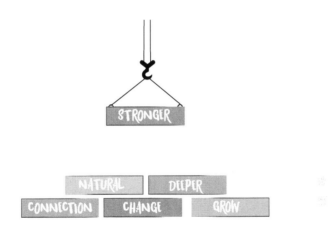

So, what exactly is happening when the dreaded, inevitable 'shift' happens? We feel like the other person is either pulling away, or it is us that feels unsure. We notice the 'good morning darling, have a great day' messages have become less frequent or stopped, and we feel like we are becoming distant from each other.

There is a big shift when our comfort level eventually builds in a relationship and we let our guard down a bit. This seems to be the perfect time for possible fear to kick in.

We wonder all the time why things have changed: 'Was it something I did wrong?' 'Did I expect too much?' 'Was I being completely unreasonable?' Or, 'Did I just have too much baggage?'. Most of the time, we are not aware of what is really going on, we just notice we feel different. We might think it is because our partner's behaviour has changed. But what could be going on is that each person's past has crept into this new relationship.

Our past fears, hurts, and childhood wounds have surfaced for more healing. If we are not aware of this, our new, wonderful, blissful relationship begins to feel just like the rest of them: disappointing, suffocating, abandoning, unsupportive, untrustworthy and unloving.

The appearance of this fear is a natural, necessary step in any relationship, and we need to embrace it rather than run away from it. This is when many relationships end, but they do not have to if both partners want to stay and build on this stage.

## Bonding phase

The fear is there as a message. It is asking to be listened to and it is a gift necessary for our own growth. When we share our fear and own that part of us, we are not blaming the other person. We do not share our fears to have the other person change or to have them fix us, but merely to allow our hearts to open up.

By owning our stuff, we are taking care of our own healing, which keeps our past from damaging the relationship in the future. It is how we clear our past patterns and allow ourselves to move forward in a new and healthy way with someone else.

The best part is that we get to see how our partners handle this as well. Our relationships need this stage and this shift from the easy, wonderful bliss because without it, our bond would never grow.

If things are easy all the time, where is the room for true, deep intimacy? How do we learn to truly support our significant others and ourselves if we never experience pain, anxiety, anger, or annoyance?

We do not, and that is why after years of being with someone, we can feel like we do not know them. If we have remained closed off and worked our hardest to keep things going smoothly, we only know that level. And the truth is there are deeper, richer, more intimate layers to us as humans and to our relationships.

Once you have opened your heart and begun communicate your fear, a small amount of vulnerability has been introduced into the relationship, and there is room for your partner to do the same. There is room for you to grow together.

Brené Brown, author and researcher, describes vulnerability as "uncertainty, risk, and emotional exposure. It's that unstable feeling we get when we step out of our comfort zone".

It is necessary to take time to get to know each other on a deeper level. All kinds of things can happen during this time, both good and bad. Time allows a relationship to build and both parties will bring their own strengths and weaknesses.

## Self-protection

There is often an early point in a new relationship that you suddenly feel vulnerable, running along with all the love chemicals we have explored. We cannot and would not want to change this, although keeping an eye on how this plays out is important.

When we allow ourselves to fall for someone, we are allowing ourselves to be vulnerable. Our minds will start to paint pictures with this person and them in our future. As we open up and reveal our inner feelings, past experiences and quirks, plus our hopes and dreams, we can start to feel a slight panic. The fear of betrayal, abandonment or rejection can slip in even though everything feels amazing.

This is particularly difficult when any past relationships have left a huge scar. If the person has been so hurt in the past, they can jump in, as we have said, to heal themselves, although another option is to start to withdraw. They may be so terrified of being hurt that they literally panic, stop responding to the other and certainly avoid starting anything serious. This can lead to someone being in a lot of new relationships, going on lots of dates although never really settling. This fear of getting close is holding them back and the old memories provide a self-protection which is almost disabling.

While it is important to protect ourselves and ensure that the new relationship is right for us, we need to be mindful of this habit.

## We construct our reality

Once we start being specific about what we want from a relationship, a partner, and how we will be, the mind is then focused. This certainly helps change our autopilot of thinking about what we do not want, usually based on past experiences. When we are clear about what we are looking for, then our attention is focused, and we are more likely to get what we want.

This works for all things in life. We need to be mindful that what we think about becomes our reality.

The mind can get to work because we set our intentions with the conscious and rational part of the mind, and then the subconscious part gets 'stuff' done. The trick to remember with the subconscious mind is that it needs clear instructions and does not do well with negative thoughts such as, 'I do not want a partner who is insecure'. The mind gets confused and does not really know what you want as the focus is in the wrong direction.

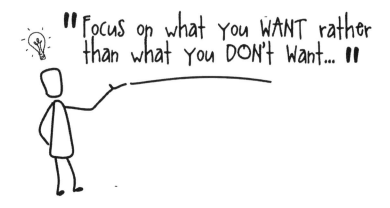

"Focus on what You WANT rather than what You DON'T Want... "

Getting serious and specific about what you want in a partner, relationship and, most importantly, how you want to be is a task that many single people neglect to spend time doing. Daring to dream about your ideal is a must! Many people can get stuck with the thinking we will call 'yearning' for someone. Sitting around yearning for someone is very different from imagining you already have them. Yearning is a feeling of 'not having', which primes us to feel desperate. We need to discourage ourselves from cultivating feelings of 'not having' and encourage ourselves to cultivate feelings of 'having'. You can easily tell the difference as the feeling of 'having' is a much better feeling!

You may say that this is just a trick of the mind, and the feelings that come as part of the package of 'lonely yearning' are tricks of the mind too. Feelings of failure, or feeling that we will never find anyone, are all part of the imagination - they are negative imaginings. This is using our mind and our imagination against us and training ourselves to fail.

## Know what you want in a relationship

The next area for us to focus on, if you want to get into a healthy, new relationship, is the need to be clear on what exactly you want from your new relationship. It is also vital to think about what you will be like in that relationship and what your partner will be like. Spending time thinking about these questions will help you attract the right person into your life, along with knowing when they have arrived.

Most people have a rough idea of what kind of person they are looking for, but what they often miss is thinking about how they will be within that relationship. This helps to ensure that you are putting your own needs, hopes and dreams into the mix, never mind making it a priority. All this will help with attracting the right person for you.

There can be a tendency to spend time focusing on what they have not got or what has not happened rather than focusing on what is there.

Here it feels right to talk about the Law of Attraction, one of the universal laws that is very powerful. The Law of Attraction is not about being attractive, as often people seem to think. It dictates that 'like attracts like'. So, for example, when a person lacks love for him or herself and feels emotional hurt or pain, they will be attracted to other people like that.

Every thought we have and every word we speak are creating our future. We construct our reality. Many people do not understand this and some even think it is ridiculous. If you can accept this, though, you can begin to deliberately create the life that you want.

With the above in mind, it is good to spend time thinking about all the qualities that both you and them will have. Once these are out of your mind and down on paper, you can check to see that you are aligned to what you are looking for. For example, you might think that you want a fit and energetic person, but the reality is you are not an outdoor person, so there would be a possible mismatch. Getting specific is key.

Secondly, and just as importantly, you need to be focused on what you want rather than what you do not want. Saying, 'I am looking for a new relationship though I do not want him to be insecure, aggressive, and indecisive', feels like you are stating what kind of a person you would like to meet. However, you are focusing on all the qualities that you do NOT want rather than what you DO want.

If you are serious about attracting the right person into your life, your task is to think about the qualities you would like them to have. This task needs to be revisited regularly as you may think of different characteristics to add which are important to you.

The second part of this powerful exercise is to ensure that you have these qualities and criteria yourself, or at least complementary qualities! We are not saying that you have to be the same as your ideal partner, though you need to be aligned.

" Most people do not get what they want simply because.... They do not know what they want. "

For example, if you would like a secure partner, you need to have addressed your own insecurity. Otherwise, you could attract a partner with your own challenges, which is exactly what you do not want.

This can be like a revolving door or the resit class for some people, and they find themselves in similar situations with the same kind of person. They repeatedly say, 'Why do I keep attracting a similar type of person?'.

Take some time now to answer the questions in the next exercise, or simply write a list of all the qualities you want in your partner.

# STEP to CHANGE

## Your Ideal Partner

# Your Ideal Partner

Take some time to reflect on your own situation.

How do you want them to be?

What key qualities should they have?

What is important about the relationship?

How do you want to feel?

How do you need to be?

Are you aligned to these qualities?

## Self-love

There is no doubt that sharing the joys and wonders of life with another person who lights up your world is priceless. As we have said already, finding this kind of happiness is hard if there is a need to be fulfilled by someone else.

"Putting yourself first is an act of self-love..."

Being needy, insecure and trying to gain approval and a sense of worth from your partner puts a huge strain on them, and it is a major turn-off.

It is an unachievable task because feeling inherently loved and worthy needs to come from within. Not from your partner.

An outstanding relationship does not come from two half-fulfilled people coming together to make one whole. This kind of relationship comes from two people coming together to share and enhance their already full and content life.

While it is important to think about what you want from a relationship and partner, as you have done in the previous exercise, it is even more important that we own and appreciate who we are and completely accept the other person for who they are too.

Putting yourself first is not selfish; it is necessary. It is imperative to happiness. Focusing on liking and loving yourself, warts and all, and knowing what you want will positively affect any relationship.

Maybe you want to feel successful or free to be yourself, which would still form an essential part of a relationship with another. If you do not prioritise this kind of thinking, then there is a high chance that you will attract a partner who is lacking and a relationship that is dissatisfying.

Take some time now to think about your own self-love, and it is important to note all the things you are not keen on too!

# STEP to CHANGE

Self-Love

# Self-Love

Take some time to reflect on your own situation.

Write down everything you love or like about yourself.

What do you have to give to a relationship?

Now be really honest with yourself....

Write down anything that you dislike so that you can work on accepting these parts.

REMEMBER - the right person will love
these things about you

# Being yourself

Have you ever noticed that it can be easier to attract a potential partner if you already have one? Have you noticed that if you are not really looking for a relationship, a lot more people show an interest, but if you get desperate, they run a mile!

Rather than just putting this down to some bizarre quirk of human nature, let us look at the cause of this behaviour and see if we can make it work for us.

One of the main reasons we often attract someone when we are not looking is because we are probably being our true self. We have nothing to prove and are owning our own space.

The key to finding a partner is to not particularly need one, or at least not need one 'too much' as this can drive them away. However, what do you do if you are really feeling desperate?

Another quirk of human nature is that our nervous system, or unconscious mind, has a hard time telling the difference between an imagined experience and a real one. This is obvious when watching an exciting or scary movie; it is as if it is real. See how easily we can fool ourselves? This is the key to never being desperate about finding a partner. If we want to find a partner, then the best thing to do is imagine we have one already!

# Imagination

It is no accident that the word 'imagination' contains the root for the word magic. *Imagination is an inner resource you can draw upon in every facet of life — a resource that, if used wisely, has the power to shape who you are, how you choose to live and what you attract into your life.*

As the subconscious mind cannot tell the difference between a real or imagined experience, mental images can virtually build a memory bank as a resource to draw upon.

If we imagine we already have the perfect partner and focus on the feelings, thoughts and behaviours, we will calm down our whole nervous system. It gives us a sense of fulfilment and takes away feelings of desperation. This is especially powerful if we really get into details; what you will do together, where you will go, what you will be saying, and how you will feel.

# Success

If this approach sounds strange to you, remember what top athletes do if they want to improve their abilities. They imagine themselves achieving a better time in the race, lifting heavier weights, having more stamina, and winning. They imagine how they will feel to achieve their goals. Top athletes do not mess around with techniques that do not work, especially when a few hundredths of a second difference means winning or losing. Successful business people do this sort of thing too, so why do we not do it with relationships?

By imagining we already have the perfect partner and how it will feel, we train our subconscious mind to start making that happen. And, because we are more likely to be mellow about it, we are much more likely to make the most of it when the next opportunity comes along. The most important part, of course, is, above all, be yourself.

Spending time developing this ideal partner will also allow you to consider all components. For example, you might be someone who thinks that they want to be romanced every day and treated like a princess. You might get that and find that it is too much! Sometimes our ideals will need to be tested in the reality, and the ideal 'checklist' is tweaked.

Thinking about these dreams is one part; writing them down strengthens it. It deepens the experience of being focused in the right way.

If you are in a position where you want to think about the type of relationship and partner you would like to attract, take time to complete this exercise. If you are already in a relationship, you can still complete it by way of refreshing your relationship, and most importantly, how you are within it.

# STEP to CHANGE

Imagine Your Perfect Partner

# Imagine Your Perfect Partner

Take some time to think about this for yourself.

What will you be doing?

What will you be saying?

What will you be thinking?

How will you be feeling?

Go back over your list and highlight all the feelings you wrote down that you already have in your life now.

Or think:

How can you feel those things in your life now?

How can you feel loved, cherished, respected, wanted?

How can you live your life as if those feelings were already true?

How can you feel like you are already in a loving relationship with your partner?

# Putting it all together

We have explored so many aspects of what makes up a relationship. It is fair to say that they are complex, and hopefully, now we know what is usually at the heart of challenges. It is so common and likely that we blame any difficulties on the other person or a situation, and yet it is just as likely to be ourselves.

It is usually 'us' who are both at the root of unhealthy difficulties, and it is, therefore, 'us' that are at the root of a healthy relationship. Both make a relationship work. By being honest, vulnerable and each taking full responsibility for themselves and their own challenges, a relationship has a great chance of success.

In the next chapter, we will be exploring some of the challenges within relationships - some inevitable and some more complex reasons.

# CHAPTER THREE

# Relationships Are Complex

In this chapter, we will explore some of the challenges that make relationships, particularly intimate ones, unhealthy. We will consider why we stay in them, what happens as a result and how we often are within one.

We need to do this first to understand what may have gone wrong in an old relationship or identify that we are in an unhealthy relationship. Either way, understanding what has happened and sorting out the 'blame' or lack of responsibility is key.

## Communication

Many of the difficulties we experience are related to communication in our relationships. It is common to hear, 'There was a breakdown in communication', or 'We hardly ever communicate how we feel', or 'It's like he/she is talking another language'. Poor communication can manifest itself into misunderstandings and misinterpretation. Any poor communication will lead to frustration, unhappiness and confusion.

## Is there a problem?

Relationships are most certainly one of the most complex things we have to navigate as humans. Relationship problems can be hard to identify, and sometimes it may be impossible for a couple to agree there is a problem in the first place. If they both agree that there is a problem, then they can begin working on it. Although if one thinks it is just a question of the other overreacting, it is difficult to make any progress at all. The ironic thing is, if a couple are not able to agree on whether they have a relationship problem, that is usually a relationship problem in itself.

Frequent conflict and anger may indicate that all is not well, and change is needed to keep the relationship healthy.

Avoiding conflict or agreeing not to talk about an issue that causes the conflict might provide short-term peace. However, it is better to sort out important relationship issues earlier rather than leaving things to fester.

Conflict is a symptom – if you patch things up without finding out what is at the bottom of your differences, you will probably find yourselves in conflict again.

Although disagreements can be unsettling, especially in the early stages of a relationship, they can deepen emotional closeness when the situation is resolved.

## Wrong match

At the beginning of our exploration of an unhealthy relationship, it is worth acknowledging that sometimes a relationship is simply the wrong match from the start. We have probably all ended up dating the wrong person - it is nothing to be ashamed of. Maybe you got swept up in the idea of how fun love seems and went for it with someone who was not right for you.

Realising that you are dating or even married to the wrong person can be the most confusing romantic problem to deal with, particularly if there are no giant, explosive red flags. While we are in the wrong relationship, we often think that the fact we are happy some of the time is proof that things are working. Often, the fact that you are a bad match only becomes clear long after you have split up – when you are trying to puzzle out what happened.

And even after we break-up, it is often hard to recognise that we could not have made things work. The other person involved was not on the same page. It is often easier to blame outside influences like work, children, family pressures, or a former partner. But despite the lack of huge alarm bells, there is often a feeling — a frequent vibe of confusion, exhaustion and general frustration with the relationship that indicates you and your partner do not have complementary personalities, values or goals, and are simply not a good match.

It is important to be able to identify a pattern in yourself when meeting a partner. We do not always fall for someone simply because their positive qualities complement our own and because their negative traits fit ours so well.

Some of the key indicators that there is a problem can be seen with too many of some things and not enough of others. There is often too much fighting, bickering and tit for tat. There is a lack of intimacy, trust and avoidance of spending much time together.

Fundamentally, both or neither's needs are being met. These are quite often emotional needs. This can be due to a lack of communication or misunderstood communication. Either has the same outcome of feeling unheard.

No matter who you are or what you are like, it is easy to find yourself stuck in a relationship that is not awful but is not really working either.

## Warning signs

It is good to be honest with yourself as early as possible and explore how a relationship is or has been for you. It is good to acknowledge these behaviours and patterns as warning signs. So often we ignore them, and yet these would be a clear indication that something is not right.

We will explore these behaviours and patterns asked in the exercise later in this chapter.

Take some time to complete this exercise for yourself. No judgement. This may help you if you are:

- possibly in an unhealthy relationship
- unsure what makes it unhealthy
- struggling to heal from a relationship that has ended, and you are still holding onto an ideal that did not exist

# STEP to CHANGE

## Warning Signs

# Warning Signs

Take a moment to think about your own situation.

Can you be your true self? Do you have to worry about what you say or how you behave in case they do not like something?

Or do you do this to your partner?

Does your partner comment, in a negative way, on what you wear or how you look or make you feel uncomfortable about these things?

Or do you do this to your partner?

Can you say how you feel or challenge them if they make statements you do not agree with?

Do you do this to your partner?

Do they have constant negative things to say about your family and friends?

Do you tend to do this?

Do you have to please them to make life easier for you? Do their needs or plans come before yours?

Do you create this situation?

## Old stories

A big player in unhealthy relationships is holding onto old stories and the guilt that may go with them. When a person is living in the past, regretting and feeling guilty, this only causes hurt and confusion; it serves no purpose. It ultimately causes pain and discomfort. Many people keep old stories alive, dwelling on what has happened in the past.

During this process, the past continues to hurt and affect the future. These uncomfortable stories keep going around and around and therefore keep the memories alive in our minds. It is as if we are constantly hitting the repeat button, and yet, in reality, it does not change the situation.

Any time focused on regrets will eat away at you emotionally and mentally and will affect a relationship. As it is affecting the person, so it naturally will affect the relationship. It is fair to say that this is true whether it is guilt from a previous relationship or something that has happened within a current one. Guilt is a destructive feature in any relationship.

As we have said, the mind is an association-making machine. It is also very focused on fairness and certainty. A past experience will mould and change us, although it is key to ensure that it does not negatively define us.

The mind will naturally live in the past if we allow it. When a relationship causes pain and hurt, we may look for someone else to blame rather than take responsibility. Or the complete opposite can happen, and we take on the whole responsibility. We often use the past as a weapon against others. We use the evidence from the past to justify or qualify our beliefs, particularly when there is conflict. It allows us to defend our position or blame another person or ourselves. As we have explored previously, this is often unhealthy as we are relying on our perception, not necessarily the reality.

## Mind reading

Another area to pay attention to is when there is a behaviour or, in fact, a habit of constantly trying to gain approval in a relationship. This can stem again from childhood, where we were trying to gain approval or attention from a parent, leaving us seeking this in our adult life. The habit of needing it becomes the challenge and realising that this is an old habit is the key to make changes.

Another behaviour that we see is trying too hard to second-guess what the other person wants. We imagine what they are thinking or feeling, and we bend over backwards to try and meet their need.

If our minds are spinning around trying to work out what we should do to 'make' our partner happy, we will become emotionally drained.

This is like 'mind reading', which, of course, is an impossible quest. How can anyone know what the best thing for another is, certainly when only using guesswork? We will continue to wind ourselves up and can often feel out of control, as no one else can settle these fears, it needs to come from within.

## Loneliness

Loneliness is a complex feeling. When someone says they feel 'lonely' in a relationship, it can mean a variety of things. Just because you are married or dating someone does not exclude the possibility of feeling lonely.

Loneliness is a sense of feeling disconnected, isolated, and disengaged from others. You can feel lonely even when you are in the same room with them. Ongoing feelings of disconnection and disengagement from your partner may be the sign that you are in a lonely relationship.

It might mean you feel unheard or unloved, or it could be a sense of confusion. It may be that something is bothering you about the relationship, and the other person either does not seem to be concerned, or there is a barrier to bringing it up.

This can feel like a terribly lonely place and can lead to other challenges if left unresolved. Feelings of loneliness can happen to anyone and at any point in their lives, in or out of a relationship. If you are feeling lonely in a marriage or relationship, it may be time to consider the reasons why and recognise the signs of a lonely relationship.

Loneliness can also create a situation where you go out of your way to please your partner, even if you know that they are not a compatible match and perhaps they even take advantage of your kind nature.

Sometimes we end up staying in destructive relationships for longer and struggle to leave because of the fear of being alone or not finding someone compatible. When you struggle to set boundaries in your relationship, it can leave you feeling frustrated, angry and anxious, and perhaps, eventually, depressed.

A lack of boundaries in relationships are unhealthy and can create many challenges. When there is a lack of boundaries, it is directly linked to difficulties of self-respect or respect for the other. An incompatible partner does not offer respect of you and your boundaries.

It is also important that you respect your own boundaries and standards. If you do not, this is a signal to the world that you are not serious about them. You will also keep attracting people that do not meet or respect your boundaries or standards.

## Heated conversations

Many couples find themselves in a constant state of war, which is distressing for both partners, and for others in and around the relationship, particularly if children are involved. There seems to be a belief in some of these couples that it is more important to win the argument and prove their point than to ensure the safety of the relationship.

Many conversations with others so easily involve some misunderstanding or misinterpretation. It is critical to keep this in mind when conversations become difficult or frustrating.

Even normal interactions may involve faulty communication; the ones with conflict often escalate. Sometimes this can lead to an even worse problem than in the first place. The higher the level of conflict, the costlier misunderstandings may be. We have all been in situations where our communication has made a difference.

Given our tendency to hear what we expect to hear, or what we interpret, it is very easy for people in conflict to misunderstand each other. In these circumstances, communication is likely to be strained, and the potential for misperceptions and misunderstandings is high.

When we go into these high emotional states, each person is unable to hear the other one clearly. This is because both are too busy getting their point across and that point is often irrational. Both are in drama with little thought of what is being said. We can also be significantly out of character, saying or doing things we would not ordinarily say or do. There are many occasions when words are interpreted as nothing like they were intended. These situations can escalate so quickly and often move away from the initial issue.

It takes a brave person to step away from this kind of argument. When emotions are high, everything seems clouded, particularly our explanations and interpretations. So often when our conversation is reflected back to us, we find ourselves responding with, 'I didn't mean it like that'.

This misinterpretation is even worse with present day electronic communication such as texts as we miss core components of communication such as eye contact, facial expression and particularly tone. In communication, we can be surprised and frustrated by the responses we get.

In calmer situations, a misunderstanding may simply be rectified with a re-explanation or repeated to be heard properly. When it truly does not work is when it has triggered off a heated conversation, causing disarray. The disagreement can result in a need to justify or defend. It is ok to have our own view and interpretation, although when we expect someone to understand us, this can cause challenges.

While we know this, we also need to keep in mind that those limiting beliefs are often being fired up and causing havoc to thoughts and feelings.

Another reason people are not good at communicating is because they do not listen to the other person! They are likely to listen passively and are often more focused on their own internal dialogue. Each person is literally formulating their answer rather than listening. Coupled with this, they are quite likely to be hearing what they think is being said. We will be looking at two different types of listening styles later in the book.

## Our past

Past experiences will impact on our interactions in any area of life, although experiences in relationships can take over. Maybe it is because we open ourselves up, or we expect more.

When things go wrong in a relationship, we are often trapped in a cycle of unhelpful analysis, as though we are watching a TV programme on repeat and keeping the pain alive. The mind keeps old stories, scenarios and conversations circulating, and many people relive and regurgitate painful stories, spending hours analysing the 'What if…?' 'If only…' or 'How could they?'.

There is very little personal growth or peace in this thinking pattern. Repeating old stories keeps the upset or negativity going. We lose our power too.

The most important aspect of this to keep in mind is that we see the world not as it is, but how we perceive it to be. In fact, as we believe it to be.

As we have explored earlier, we see, feel and understand the world through our own personal lens, which means that our view will be very different from everyone else, making each of us unique. Just like we all have our own fingerprints, we also have our own way of processing and understanding the world.

We are all able to distort or muddle up what has been said or done, which has a huge and varied effect on our responses. It is this uniqueness that causes many of the communication problems between people. It is virtually impossible to truly understand something from another's perspective but knowing that allows us to be more flexible and accommodating.

The outcome frequently is that we can get trapped in a habit of blaming others rather than taking responsibility and ownership. When blaming others, we are focused externally and say, 'He said/she said,' or 'He did/she did'. This often means we are locked into the details of the situation and generally repeating the cycle. The relationship or situation will continually be in trouble with constant unrest or misunderstandings. The trap becomes that each person is adamant that the other person is at fault.

## Values

Our values are what are important to us. Values act as an internal guidance system, and when all is well, these are at the heart of every major decision we make, even if we are unaware that this is happening. How we view and experience our world through the current 'frame' is very much influenced by our values.

Our values are a key driver of happiness and fulfilment in life. They are unique to each of us and there is no right or wrong about them. They are integral, and what is an important value to one, is not necessarily for another. Although we all share values, as many of them make the human world function, we often attach our own meaning to them.

Our values are important because they help us grow and develop. They help us create the future we want to experience. We all make hundreds of decisions every day. Every decision we make and everything we say and do reflects our values and beliefs. When we use our values to make decisions, we make a deliberate choice to focus on what is important to us.

When we make choices that fulfil our values, we are more likely to feel content and satisfied. For example, when you have a value around love and your partner demonstrates love in a way that you understand and accepts your efforts, then this value is being fulfilled. You will see your relationship as satisfying your values. When love is demonstrated in a way that does not fit with your model of the world, this is when we can get into difficulties. Understanding each other's interpretations can make such a difference.

## Shared values

A couple can have shared values in their relationship such as love, trust, honesty, commitment and respect. However, the understanding is very personal to each person and, as we have explored, could have a different interpretation.

It is often asked: 'Can a relationship be successful if the couple have different values?'. Values can play out heavily when relationships are in trouble, although creating an environment where there is an understanding of each other's values is a must.

It is a good approach to spend time ensuring that the interpretation of a shared value or other values is explored. For example, a couple might know that they both value love. However, they have a slightly different idea about how this will be shown. One might feel that they are showing love in caring ways like making the meals, while the other shows love by saying it. This can cause a challenge due to expectations and not understanding each other's behaviours.

We often expect someone to behave as we do, and this then causes conflict. No two people are the same, having this level of expectation is unrealistic. Challenges will occur when these differences are not spoken about. When there are healthy conversations, both can feel understood, and there can be a change in behaviour to support the other. Making this kind of change may require patience and appreciation.

A positive approach is for each person to first identify what is important to them in relation to their relationship — then having an open discussion about the potentially different meanings, interpretations and how they can be demonstrated. This way there are no surprises, and it avoids the risk of discontentment. Each understands what is important and how they are fulfilled.

## Neglecting and violating values

We have explored that we will feel content when our values are being fulfilled, although something that is usually out of our awareness is when our unhappiness comes from not living by these values. We become very unhappy when our values are not fulfilled. We can often neglect them ourselves or allow someone to violate them.

If we commit any time or energy to something that neglects or violates our core values, we start to feel resentment and frustration. When we are not honouring our values in our choices, there will be a nagging within that something is missing or wrong in our lives. In many situations, when you feel angry, frustrated or stuck, there is a high chance that you are not living through your values. You are likely to ignore or neglect what is important to you or allow your values to be violated.

As this is out of our awareness, the tendency is to think that the unhappiness is linked to another person or situation. We then blame someone or something rather than look within and realise that we have put ourselves in a situation that has challenged our own values.

In these types of situations, you need to focus on what is happening within you and not get fixated on the behaviour of others. This could be one of those lessons you very much need, and action is required.

Firstly, it is useful to identify and know what your values around relationships are. Then you can establish if you are fulfilling them, using them in healthy decisions, or whether you are neglecting them or allowing a person or situation to violate them.

Understanding and knowing your values can help you know when someone else is driving you and the relationship.

You can run this exercise in another context if you wish, like career, health & fitness or life in general, though focus on relationships initially.

# STEP to CHANGE

Your Values

# Your Values

Take a moment to think about your own situation.

Ask yourself, in the context of relationships, what is important?

List everything that pops into your mind. Keep asking yourself the same question until you come up with a huge list of your values.

Examples are trust, love, honesty, loyalty, connection, sharing, passion.

Now with this list, consider these questions:

- Do you fulfil them?

How?

- Do you neglect them?

How?

- Are they violated?

How?

# Changing in relationships

It is a myth that people or relationships do not change. It is inevitable. Relationships go through different developmental stages and situations which create change. It is natural for changes to occur.

Good communication between a couple will allow change to happen in a healthy way. If there are changes that are needed or desired, then this needs to be managed well, respectfully and in agreement.

Of course, we will make changes ourselves as the years go on and, in most relationships, we all grow and develop over time. We can learn so much about ourselves when we meet new people. We then evolve and change through different people, although this needs to be changes that are right for each person. In close intimate relationships, we are more likely to see our own behaviours, which we might want to address. However, the closer we get to being with the person that is right for us, the less changes are needed. If someone really loves you, that person will love you exactly as you are.

Many people stay in bad relationships with the desire to change their partner. You may be the one hoping or trying to change someone else. This is not a good place to be and will cause major issues. We all want to be loved for who we are, and sometimes we forget and secretly hope that the other person will change some of themselves! When you are focused on changing your partner, you miss the opportunity to work together to come up with a solution. This must come from each person who wants to change, not the other way around.

## Changing you

We have already explored the positives and challenges with a new relationship. Remember, it is important to acknowledge that making changes within yourself solely to try and make a relationship work does not always end well. These kinds of changes can be a betrayal to yourself.

When people try to change to be with someone else or to fit in, we are less likely to be ourselves. Take Danny and Sandy from 'Grease'. Each thought that they needed to change their style and outlook to get the attention of the other. If you remember in the story, they had been happy with each other as they were during the summer when they first met early in the film. We can find ourselves trying to change our behaviour, values, looks, and even personality if we believe it means pleasing the other person or being liked.

As mentioned before, through others we can see behaviours we want to change, or a relationship can create a safe environment to explore limiting thoughts and beliefs and we become more confident. This is all healthy and positive because it is something that we want to do. The danger zone is if we try and change so that someone will love us.

Take some time and space to reflect on this. Be honest and non-judgemental with yourself.

# STEP to CHANGE

## Where Are You?

# Where Are You?

Take some time to think about your own situation.

- Are you making changes to be loved?

- What are you doing?

- Are you trying too hard?

- How are you trying too hard?

- Are your behaviours driven by a fear?


- What unhealthy behaviours have you noticed?


- Are you trying to change someone else?


- What are you noticing?

## Equal investment

There are so many kinds of imbalance that can show up in a relationship. Some are positive and can create a yin/yang. Differences can be enhancing although they can so easily cause difficulties.

It is natural to want to be invested in a relationship. Relationships are often more complicated than we give them credit for, and sometimes it can feel like one partner seems more invested than the other. No two people will love each other with perfect equality or in the same way. However, a problem can come when there is a clear imbalance of love within the relationship. In these instances, it can feel like one is putting in more effort or the only one taking the relationship seriously. This is where it can feel unfair and becomes unhealthy. If there is an imbalance, then there is a risk that this will cause greater problems further down the line.

Some find themselves in a situation where they have invested too much and drop everything to see their partner, even though this is not reciprocated. One person may be unwilling to change their plans or inconvenience themselves for the sake of the relationship.

Another difference is when one partner does not consider the other when making plans. They seem to be doing things without any discussion, which for another can feel alien because sharing plans is seen as an important part of the relationship. It can cause problems as it can be interpreted as hurtful, inconsiderate and can trigger limiting beliefs. These simple differences can be seen by another as an issue around investment.

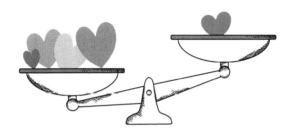

In many relationships, it may be that one person is better at planning than the other. Some are naturally good at planning, and it can work well with some couples. However, it can cause conflict if it is too imbalanced. While planning is not everyone's strengths, it is important for both parties to feel like the other shows a commitment and makes some plans, especially a lovely surprise. It is also worth noting that some people say that they are 'never' allowed to plan anything, or if they do, it is not good enough.

When one party is not as invested, there is a risk of a physical or emotional affair starting. They may be looking to have their needs met outside the relationship. If you were invested, you would not dream of it. People may not be cheating physically, but they may be involved with someone else emotionally and quite often they do not see the issue. If there is a private relationship with someone else, then this is likely to cause an issue.

Sometimes it is just a little nagging feeling that is not necessarily tied to something deeper. It might be that your partner is stressed at work and has not realised it is affecting the relationship.

Another sign that there is a problem is when it feels like one party is holding back and will not fully let their partner in. This can often be associated with past hurt and a fear of being hurt again.

Some have a partner isolated in a small segment of their life. Or they could be bored, distracted or are not aware that they are doing this. Some of our behaviours are out of our awareness and therefore reside in a blind spot. We have already explored this interesting point earlier.

## Time invested

Many of us feel the need to 'see something through', especially when we have invested emotionally. This behaviour is ingrained in us and it can even be a necessity to stick at something we started. Personal investment has a high regard, and we often protect things because of this. This is obviously not true for everyone and we will certainly all have stories of things that we gave up on too easily!

When we start a relationship, we certainly do not enter it to end it. When we have invested time, energy and our hearts, we are very likely to want to keep trying. While trying is positive, couples often keep trying in the same way as before and therefore nothing changes.

Something that we would all love to keep is that initial feeling when we first fall in love. More established relationships develop into something else and at a deeper level. One trap to find yourself in is wishing it were like it was at the beginning and this can put a great deal of pressure on a relationship. We have already explored the highs and lows of a new love.

## Expression

It is important and generally healthy to be able to talk about needs and express feelings. As we have explored, we cannot assume that anyone else sees the situation the same. Some people are not very good at sharing what is on their mind, while others are the complete opposite. Some may share all their internal chatter, which is not particularly formed and unlikely to be helpful to the relationship. There is no doubt that how each person manages personal emotions and the behaviour to follow will differ. These differences can be out of our awareness and, therefore, can cause conflict.

A longer-term relationship can need a re-boot of energy. This often needs to be a conscious effort as it is easy to fall into a 'rut'. Here the risk is taking each other for granted and becoming complacent. The trick is often a tweak in communication and/or a space to be able to express feelings and needs.

## Children

Children in a relationship naturally have an impact. In this book, we will be taking a brief look at how children affect a relationship and, most specifically, staying in unhealthy ones. It is fair to say that children will bring a great deal of joy and also challenges.

One key pointer is that children usually do not help a relationship that is already challenging. The notion that a baby will fix any cracks in a relationship is usually a misconception.

In this section, we will take a brief look at the impact of staying in unhealthy relationships for the sake of the children.

Children obviously can create a wonderful bond and be the best thing to happen to a couple. Equally, the possibility of pre-existing cracks can become bigger. Children can also get caught in the conflict, be used as pawns or a threat. Children being in the middle of any adult conflict is not healthy.

It is not uncommon to stay in a relationship for the sake of children. The challenge here is to shield children from any conflict and arguing. The implied message is that children are better off being raised in an intact family, spared from the effect of divorce. This position requires deep consideration.

It is worth considering whether people do stay together for the sake of the children or are fearful of coming to terms with their own challenges. It is also worth checking that we are not trying to avoid larger fears.

The effects of remaining in an intact family where the parents are either in conflict or simply loveless should also be considered.

In marriages where there is anger, conflict or marked unhappiness, children are witnessing this as 'the norm'. As adults, children are likely to replicate a relationship modelled on their parents. We want to teach them to be kind, loving, forgiving and to believe in themselves. Often, this kind of situation does not demonstrate that. We tell children that they deserve healthy, respectful and loving relationships, although these situations demonstrate the opposite. The parents lack the courage to see this for themselves.

Often, people are afraid to move on with their lives and take responsibility for their own happiness. Financial concerns or a fear of being alone often create paralysis and hide beneath a mask of false togetherness for the children's sake. This can also be for the sake of other family members and to save face.

In these circumstances, unloving or conflicted marriages or relationships can follow a lineage and are passed down from generation to generation.

Research indicates that most children adapt to their new circumstances within a few years. Having two parents successfully move forward with their lives teaches an invaluable lesson - that we deserve to be happy and to feel loved. Conversely, remaining in relationships that perpetuate anger, doubt, and lack of positive interactions leaves an indelible scar on children.

## Time to reflect

We have had a chance to look at many of the common features and reasons for an unhealthy relationship. Some of these will have resonated with you. It is now time to stop and think about a relationship that has not worked out for you. Take some to reflect and use the questions in the next exercise.

# STEP to CHANGE

## Your Reflections

**Your Reflections**

Take a moment to think about your own situation.

Why didn't this relationship work out?

What part did I play?

What part did they play?

What was I/they putting up with that was unacceptable?

What was I/they not challenging that was actually acceptable?

What was I/they not doing?

In the next chapter, we will look at some of the reasons and behaviours associated with unhealthy and more challenging relationships. It is worth remembering that these behaviours can come in varying degrees of severity and frequency, although understanding them is useful either way.

We will also look at a model which is helpful to understand the behaviours we can all adopt when things are not working out for us.

# CHAPTER FOUR

# Challenges in Relationships

# Drama – pulled into old stories and patterns

It is important to remember that the mind holds onto all memories, both positive and negative and this is natural and part of our protection. Taking time and space to work on freeing yourself from the impact of negative experiences and reduce their influence in your future is critical.

Keeping old painful experiences alive is destructive. It is these stories, which the mind has often exaggerated or distorted, that we need to leave in the past as a set of memories rather than a living reality. In a relationship, keeping these old stories going affect the process of moving on, particularly emotionally but can also influence any new relationship. The impact of the old stories will play out in a new or current relationship in a variety of ways.

Working through and letting go of what has happened in the past, helps to free you to be present. Otherwise, the risk is that old patterns and habits could repeat themselves. This will also mean that they define you and your ability to be a good partner. This is obviously true for someone you are in a relationship with.

Allowing old memories to become a comfortable part of the past (yes, even the horrendous ones) is far better than reliving them.

## Drama Triangle

A great model to help us understand conflict in relationships is called the *Drama Triangle* (Stephen Karpman). We tend to get into drama when it is not going our way, when we feel unhappy, and we have usually put the blame onto the behaviours of another, or ourselves, unfairly.

We can use this model to helps us to unpack relationships. We can then name the behaviours through the roles, and we can also make more sense of the situation, our own behaviours, that of others and therefore improve the situations with the others.

There are three positions on the drama triangle:

- The victim
- The persecutor
- The rescuer

The names of the roles help us to describe traits and give us a language to make sense of some complicated situations. Just for clarity, the name victim is not to be confused with someone who has experienced unreasonable or traumatic events. Equally, the persecutor does not just mean someone who is aggressive.

It is helpful to first identify each role's characteristic and then understand the behaviours in a relationship. Seeing these behaviours will help you to understand what is or has been holding you back. And this then helps you to grow and develop.

## The roles

Within all relationships in life, we can adopt any position on the drama triangle, although they can play out more heavily in an intimate relationship. In any situation, we can put ourselves into the positions or be pulled in by another.

The roles within the drama triangle, once understood, help us to look at challenging situations and relationships through a different lens. We will look at the general traits first and then we can dig a little deeper to link them to intimate relationships.

When we are at war emotionally, it is obvious that each partner's main aim is to defend their own position - in some cases, inflicting the maximum amount of damage to 'the enemy'. The use of language in these situations can often indicate that there is no truce: 'His behaviour is so selfish,' or 'She is being completely unreasonable'.

The problem with this kind of situation is that both parties feel like a victim and the other is the persecutor. Each partner sees their own behaviour as acting out of self-defence, while the other interprets the same behaviour as unprovoked aggression. This leads to a stalemate.

## Victim role - 'Why does this keep happening to me?'

A victim is someone who usually feels overwhelmed by their own sense of vulnerability, inadequacy or powerlessness. They do not take responsibility for themselves or safeguard their own power.

Whether we knowingly admit it or not, most of us react to life as victims. There are a lot of influences which force people to think that they are at the effect of something. It clearly is not a good place, although we can all be caught in it. We often feel badly done by or we believe that things are done to us.

Victim thinking can prevent us from taking responsibility for ourselves. Life is unfair and things keep happening to us. Victims tend to believe that they are powerless to make any changes and are not worthy, good enough or weaker than another person. This creates feelings of hurt, fear, and a sense of being stuck.

As a result, victims often find themselves either people-pleasing, blaming or punishing themselves, having lower self-esteem, being needy or believing people are superior or better than them. All these behaviours are coming from a place of fear and become a way to gain some relief. 'Either feel sorry for me, or I will feel sorry for myself'.

Because of another person's actions, a victim can take the stance that, 'Things never work out for me', and 'It is all my fault'. From this position, there is a tendency to interpret a lot of what others say as a criticism or take comments personally.

In some situations, a victim can feel so low about themselves that they often see others as more powerful and controlling. A victim can build resentment, which can manifest itself into retaliation and then the positions can rotate. The victim then becomes a perpetrator, blaming the other person.

Being a victim can become part of our identity and, even though destructive, it is a strange sort of comfort zone. It becomes familiar and, in some instances, we only know ourselves with these negative beliefs and thoughts.

A relationship can then be formed with a perpetrator who treats us as we believe we deserve. Sometimes we internalise the feelings, which eats away at us. Ultimately, we get stuck and do not have the life we want.

Victim thinking can keep us stuck in the resit class, which happens when we are not looking and learning from experiences and taking a vital lesson for ourselves. In these situations, we need to be open and acknowledge our own responsibility.

For a victim to feel better, they may seek out a rescuer to take care of them - someone who will listen to our stories and feel sorry for us. The rescuer, though well-meaning, is likely to offer their advice which to the victim can feel overwhelming. The victim could move to the persecutor position and persecute their rescuer. A victim will always feel like a victim until they take responsibility for themselves.

A victim's behaviour can be:

- Self-blame
- Hopelessness
- Comparing self to others
- Worry thinking
- Indecisiveness
- Fear of disappointment
- Fear of rejection
- Seeking approval & permission
- Saying sorry too often

## Reliance on a partner (Victim)

Frequently in relationships, when a self-limiting belief is running the show, there can be a reliance on someone else to complete your identity and 'make you happy'. This not only puts a great deal of pressure on the relationship but is also giving away an enormous amount of personal power.

We would all like to make our partners happy — that's part of the joy of being in a relationship. But if your partner actively believes that it is your job (and is disappointed in you when you do not succeed) to make them happy, it might be time to think long and hard about where things are going.

We can be governed by our need for security, approval, recognition and acceptance. Many people feel that being in a relationship or having loads of friends completes them - could this be you or someone you know?

Many people place their own happiness dependent on another person or a situation changing. This is a fragile position to be in. We can fall into a trap of believing that everything will be fine when something happens. This type of thinking leads people to say statements like:

• Everything will be good when I have a partner.

• Everything will be fine when we are married.

 • Everything will be ok when we live together.

• Everything will be ok when we move to a new house.

When you rely heavily on someone else or something changing, this is not only pressure, but a huge risk of a let-down. Other people or a situation do not have this power; it can only come from within. While a person or a change of circumstance can enhance your life, it is not the deep answer.

Here is a case study to use as an example of this kind of situation.

Jake is in a fairly new relationship with Kelly. They both live with their respective parents and have been seeing a lot of each other. They have been chatting on the phone for hours over the past few months. This makes Jake feel very secure and when he is not with Kelly or talking to her, he becomes anxious.

His thoughts are beginning to be very irrational, thinking that she does not want to be with him. He imagines that she is not even thinking about him, even though there is no evidence of this.

He is in his room pacing the floor, constantly checking his phone. He is searching through social media, looking for any proof that might back up his fears. He is starting to panic, even feeling sick on occasions. He is starting to think that he must have done something wrong to upset her. He is unable to concentrate on anything meaningful.

The next minute, Kelly calls and Jake is instantly settled. It is as if all his fears are gone in a moment and he is able to chat freely with her. He does ask a lot of questions about what she has been doing, although her call has settled him.

The reliance on Kelly calling to settle Jake is the exact situation we want to avoid. He was not able to settle himself, and by allowing himself to become more agitated with the lack of contact, he could have caused a bigger issue.

The position he had got himself into may have resulted in him being offhand or even angry with Kelly. This also would be very damaging for the relationship.

Have a think about this for yourself.

What would you advise Jake to do next time if a similar situation arises?

What could Jake do to reduce the possibility of a similar situation arising?

## Fear of disappointment

The fear of being a disappointment to someone, particularly a partner, can be at the root of challenging relationships. This can be coupled with interpreting that you are a failure and are unable to get anything right. By living in fear of causing disappointment or getting it wrong, you are likely to make decisions that are not right for you in the hope of pleasing others.

Within a relationship, when unhappiness has started, there can be an assumption that someone has done something wrong. There are many behaviours we can expect: such as tiptoeing around, overcompensating, anticipating a blow-up or becoming critical or defensive.

## Fear of rejection

We are shaped by our experiences as children and as we grow up. We can adopt a fear of rejection from the way we were parented, which leads us to believe that all people will reject us. These fears are often unconscious and certainly deep-rooted and show up once we feel love for ourselves. Our model of love is also created from our childhoods and this can and will affect our ability to feel safe in a relationship.

Being in a relationship is one of the most vulnerable positions you can be in, and a fear of rejection is natural. You have to put your trust and faith in the arms of another person and hope that they will reciprocate your love for them.

Those with a fear of rejection often have difficulty expressing their own needs or standing their ground. There may also be feelings of jealousy or distrust in a partner as the fear of rejection turns into a fear of being abandoned. This can have a detrimental impact on any relationships or can be the reason behind the lack of them.

Humans have a deep need to belong and connect with others, both romantically and otherwise. It is linked to our need for emotional security and our sense of belonging.

A fear of rejection can sabotage a relationship and cause constant conflict. A behaviour often seen when it becomes a saboteur, is ending a relationship as it starts to get more serious or at a first argument. The protective thinking is, 'This is it! She or he will leave me now. I had better break-up the relationship'.

Fearing rejection and ending a relationship can become a cycle and often at the heart of a list of unsuccessful relationships. This pattern could be stopping a relationship from having a chance. The fear of rejection is literally driving the relationship. There can be a constant break-up/make up cycle, which is unhealthy, though, more importantly, the fear of rejection is not addressed properly.

Fear of rejection in relationships can take many forms. It can destroy intimate relationships or prevent one from happening. Ultimately, we all want to be loved and accepted as we are, but in close relationships, we need to learn to live with the fear of rejection.

Here are a few ideas to consider:

- Accept that you have this fear
- Validate your feelings, it is ok
- Look for lessons for yourself
- Know your worth
- Reach out to others
- Avoid negative self-talk

When in a victim role, you can attract people who will treat you as you believe you deserve. They may be controlling, or a drain to your resources and this seems to be out of your control. In this situation, it is common to jump into a position of blaming the other person or being annoyed with them. This moves you into the next position on the drama triangle —the persecutor. These behaviours will only drain you and fill you with negativity.

Taking responsibility comes from noticing that you are 'in drama'. You are likely to be attracting them into your life and this will continue until you are able to see your own behaviour.

## Persecutor role – 'It's their fault'

The persecutor believes that other people are to blame and that they need to change to make things better.

Persecutors can seek out a victim to blame and are unaware of their blaming tactics. They feel that attack is warranted and necessary for self-protection as they usually believe that their way is the only way. They subsequently think or say things like: 'She is useless'. 'He does it deliberately'. 'You're doing it all wrong'. Or, 'You should have known better'. They can easily justify their vengeful behaviour. 'They asked for it'. 'They got what they deserved'. Or 'It was their fault anyway'.

Even though their actions are usually somewhat aggressive, they often feel that the world is dangerous, and people cannot be trusted, so they think, 'I need to get them before they hurt me'.

Persecutors can present more passively too; it is not always an aggressive approach. The position of persecutor is synonymous with being unaware of one's own power and therefore discounting it. Either way, the power used is negative and often destructive.

Any person within the drama triangle may at any time switch roles. However, their own internal perception may be that they are being persecuted and become the victim. There are, of course, instances in which the persecutor is knowingly and maliciously persecuting the other person. Persecutors can spend their lives in a tense, perpetual cringe against the next blow or the next crisis and are sure that there is always a missile of bad luck lurking with their name on it, about to hit its mark.

Like a victim, they can take comments personally or interpret them as criticism. They can genuinely believe that the other people are wrong, and they blame them for difficulties. The behaviours, which fit well with this position, can include being right, being negative, being critical or judgemental. All because they are not prepared to look at themselves and see their part in the situation.

While we all have a set of principles within us and a strong sense of right and wrong, persecutors can portray this quite forcefully. They often place a strong set of principles on themselves and others. They begin to judge other's actions and get annoyed because they are not meeting their standards. The response can be expressed as anger, jealousy or self-pity – 'How could they have done that to me?'.

A persecutor's behaviour can be:


- Constant criticism
- Always being right
- Defensiveness
- Punishing others
- Insecurity
- Jealousy
- Stubbornness
- Arrogance

## Critical

Often at the heart of this kind of negativity is a lack of self-love. It is often driven by a fear of being disrespected by others, of not being loved, or a fear that bad things are going to happen.

Quite often, when the above is happening, partners and others are often in the firing line for negative comments. When we feel rubbish inside, it is common to lash out at others and be overly critical. This is common in intimate relationships when there is a lack of self-love.

When a person makes negative comments, they may be using this to feel better about themselves (a type of limiting belief). Whether this is to knock everything down to their level or to boost their own ego by feeling smart and capable by noticing the flaws. The defence mechanism is to be negative, risk-averse and often mistrusting. For some, their past experiences have created a belief that the world is a disappointing and negative place, so they criticise others as a coping mechanism.

Problems come when we tip into righteousness, resistance, anger, fault-finding or badgering.

Criticism in a relationship is a behaviour that can be toxic to the couple. It erodes away positive feelings over time and leads to other problematic behaviours that can destroy the connection. Criticism in relationships occurs when we focus on our partner's flaws and pass judgement. Constant criticism is a sign that someone is unhappy, although what is often missed is that this is usually with themselves. It is most certainly a probable signal that the relationship is also in some difficulty.

When someone is happy in themselves and their relationship, they do not complain about their partner all the time. That said, it is known that we are hardest and harshest to our nearest and dearest. There are behaviours and conversations which go on within relationships and families, which would rarely happen in other friendships.

Sometimes this behaviour has become a habit within the relationship, or it could be a mirror to a parent's relationship witnessed as a child. Either way, the task at the moment is to notice if this resonates with you.

## Insecurities

Insecurity is a reality for all of us on one level or another. Some is good to an extent because it makes couples work harder in the relationship and value each other.

However, when there is too much insecurity, it can create a toxic atmosphere in the relationship and can wreak havoc on confidence and trust. It can even separate partners who love and care for each other.

Feelings of insecurity can be linked to poor self-image and lack of self-confidence. At worst, there is a strong possibility of jealousy. We will explore this further a little later.

When a person finds themselves feeling anxious about a relationship, this is a sure sign that something needs some attention. There is a double issue when they feel afraid to bring it up and talk about their feelings with their partner. There can be a fear that they will come across as needy or insecure. It might be that they think they are difficult and then the fear-based behaviours present which could cause the relationship to end.

This internal feeling could be linked to a limiting belief rather than a reality, although real things do happen to relationships. Remember that the mind can process things incorrectly. This affects self-worth and beliefs and may be interpreted as rejection. It can result in someone thinking: 'I am not worthy'. 'I'm not special'. Or, 'I do not deserve to be happy'.

The impact of limiting beliefs, such as, 'I am not good enough', or those above, are evident in relationships that are not settled. It may not be the relationship that is challenged, but the person struggling to see good in themselves. There is a likelihood that the behaviours will include either pushing away or sabotaging, which support the idea that: 'I am not worthy', or, 'I don't deserve'.

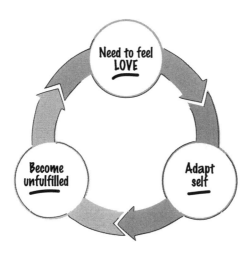

It is normal to want to be with the person you are in the relationship with. When you are in love, you do not need to see the person to feel safe. If you need to see the other person to understand how they feel, this is a problem. When you only feel safe when you are together, it is more like an attachment than a relationship.

Check out this case study describing a relationship where insecurity is playing out and blame is being used as the root.

Remember, no judgement. We are just noticing at this stage.

CASE STUDY

Matthew and Lisa have been colleagues and friends for years. They have socialised with each other and shared stories about previous relationships. They start going out and form a closer relationship.

Matthew starts to notice that he felt concerned when Lisa was going out with her friends. Lisa was finding all the questions such as 'where she is going', 'who will be there' and other similar queries as too intense. She goes along with reassuring Matthew at the start of the relationship although starts to feel unsettled quickly.

Matthew finds his mind is racing, thinking that Lisa is not being truthful and making up stories in his head. He starts to get very anxious whenever they are apart and is only settled when he speaks to her. He even finds himself checking up on her.

His insecurities are linked to an old relationship where he was unfaithful are playing out. His emotions get the better of him and he starts to suffocate the relationship.

Lisa had never seen this behaviour when they were friends, and she is shocked. Conversations become intense, she feels accused of not being truthful and yet she has nothing to hide.

All the stories were in Matthew's head and were triggering his own doubt and insecurities. He made up stories which caused them both problems.

The risk is always to blame the other for the difficulties rather than looking for the root cause.

# Jealousy

Some jealousy that is managed well can actually be healthy. Healthy jealousy can cause people to be considerate of how their actions affect their partner. It can show a commitment and a depth to the relationship.

Obviously, there is a darker side to this, which is very closely linked to insecurities and limiting beliefs.

Jealousy and suspicion, particularly if acted on to an extreme, can put an end to a relationship. Doubt can be playing out when rationally there is no reason or evidence. This is a sure sign of unhealthy jealousy. Sometimes it can be linked to past experiences and a fear that this could happen again. For example, you have been cheated on in the past and you worry this will happen again. Your mind works overtime, and you imagine that they are with someone else. When you speak to them, you may accuse your partner for which you have no evidence for. Over time the risk is your partner will feel mistrusted and even angry. Because doubt is in the mind, another difficulty is that no level of reassurance will settle you, so there are lots of negative conversations which feel like you are going around in circles.

Some people glamourise jealousy and excuse it by saying it is a sign of love. This is an unhealthy route of love. It is a sign of insecurity and reflective of seeing a partner as an object to be possessed. It is a negative emotion stemming from both desire and insecurity but unlikely to be healthy love.

Jealousy can rear its head in any relationship. It is usually a destructive emotion. It has the potential to suffocate a happy partnership and break down the trust that was there. Jealousy can cause you to experience a range of feelings, from insecurity and suspicion to rejection, fear, anger or anxiety.

It is a misconception that people get jealous because of the way someone else behaves. Unless, of course, someone has done something that is deemed unacceptable within the relationship, such as having an affair. Jealousy is not about the way 'he talked to her' or because of the way 'she smiled at him'. Jealousy is like most of the other emotions; it comes from within.

A big part of the problem lies within you and not with the person you are jealous of. When people are self-assured, they are unlikely to suffer with jealously, although not always. It can be so complex. So, let us have a look at some of the causes of jealousy.

The main cause for feeling jealousy is self-doubt. This can be linked to your abilities or skills, although often it is just how you see yourself. Jealousy can be driven by low self-esteem or a poor self-image. For example, if you think that you are ugly or unattractive, then there is a chance there will be an issue whenever you meet someone who you think looks better than you. Another dynamic is when you do not feel attractive and confident, it can be hard to believe that your partner truly loves and values you. When someone is afraid in their relationship, their fear may be that they will end up alone or be rejected and this thinking can lead to jealousy.

Other times, jealousy can be caused by unrealistic expectations about the relationship.

When someone becomes jealous, they may start to invade the private space of their partner. This can result in relationship dissatisfaction for the one whose private space is invaded.

Other signs of a jealous partner are:

- wanting to be in touch 24/7
- stalking social media
- paranoid about a phone
- having an issue when you mention someone else
- making it difficult to see friends or family
- causing an issue when going out without them

They are often misinterpreting their partner's actions and creating stories in their head, which fit with how they feel rather than the reality. The need to know every detail of a partner's life or where they are all the time can be conveyed as an expression of love and affection, although there is no space in this kind of relationship.

The longer-term effects of jealousy can include a decrease in one's perceived self-worth, emotional instability, feelings of bitterness, the break-up of relationships, prolonged depression and extreme anxiety. Emotions are temporary, but actions can be irrevocable.

Although this does not mean that every jealous person will become abusive, it does mean that jealousy is an unhealthy trait in a relationship and something you should keep an eye on. We will be looking at relationships which have become abusive later in the book.

As we have explored the causes of jealousy, it highlights the importance of individuals working on themselves first, freeing their self-limiting beliefs, building their own self-esteem and confidence and actually liking themselves before embarking on a relationship.

Check out this case study which describes a relationship where insecurity is playing out.

Check to see if this resonates with you or a relationship you have been in, or indeed, are in now.

Remember, no judgement. We are just noticing at this stage.

Ruth and Louise are in a relationship. Louise has issues with trust and believes that Ruth is constantly going to finish the relationship and find someone else.

Ruth hardly sees her friends now and is also very careful who she spends time with. She spends a lot of time reassuring Louise when she is going out or when she is particularly unsettled.

Ruth makes excuses or cancels arrangements at the last minute for an easier life. Ruth has become terrified of the negative response and arguments if she does her own thing – she is not getting on with her own life.

She has to build herself up to tell Louise that she has been invited out with her friends, fearing the consequences.

The reality is not helping Louise. These insecurities are ruling all parts of their relationship. She is not addressing the root of her insecurities or at least acknowledging that she has a problem. She is expecting Ruth to always be with her so that she feels safe.

They spend hours on the phone when apart; Ruth usually reassuring Louise as she is interpreting actions through her fear thinking. It is her responsibility to address her doubt rather than Ruth's responsibility to change her life or walk on eggshells to keep her happy.

As with any of the positions of the drama triangle, there is a risk that situations will be misinterpreted, and it is these misinterpretations that cause the most conflict. There is blame and very little reflection on what is actually causing the problem.

## Rescuer role - 'I'll save you'

Within the drama triangle, the less obvious position is that of the rescuer. This can be just as unhealthy as the other positions. They are likely to believe they must help others and will look to help a specific person or type of person. Their approach to helping and supporting can be disempowering, and it trains people to take up or be held in the victim role. A rescuer is someone who often does not own their vulnerability and seeks instead to 'rescue' those whom they see as vulnerable.

The traits of a rescuer are that they often do, or believe they do, more than 50 percent of the work. They may offer help unasked, rather than find out if or how the other person wants to be supported. What the rescuer agrees to do may, in actual fact, not be what the victim is asking for, nor what is good for the rescuer. This means that the rescuer may often feel hard done by, resentful, used or unappreciated in some way.

The rescuer does not take responsibility for themselves but instead likes to take responsibility for the perceived victim. The rescuer usually ends up feeling like the victim, but sometimes may be perceived by others, who are on the outside looking in, as being the persecutor because they can be quite bossy or demanding. The rescuer can smother, control and manipulate others, believing, 'It's for their own good'. They want to 'fix' the victim and gain personal achievement by feeling valued and worthwhile.

Their behaviours can pacify the persecutor and then build up resentment towards them. The huge risk for the rescuer is they are likely to burn out because what they are doing is not sustainable. An inevitable outcome is to eventually take the position of the victim - 'No matter how much I do, it's never enough'.

Just to clarify, the rescuer position is different from someone who is supporting or offering wanted guidance. We can be a helpful friend or partner, as long as the other person has asked for help or advice! Even then, your advice may not be right for the other person. It may be good advice, but the victim may not be ready or does not want to hear it (some people stay in victim mode and are unable to take action for themselves).

A rescuer's behaviour can be:

- seeking approval & permission
- saying yes
- people-pleasing
- disempowering others
- taking unnecessary responsibility
- burnout
- making assumptions/mind-reading

We all want to take responsibility for ourselves rather than be 'fixed' by someone else, which can feel disempowering. In some dynamics, a person is permanently in the rescuer position within a relationship or family. They are expected to do everything, come up with all the solutions and generally be there for everyone else. When we see this in younger years, a behaviour pattern can form where the rescuer is so busy looking out for everyone else that they are then unsure of who they are and will certainly not be getting what is right for them.

Being aware of the positions on the drama triangle helps to step back, think, and respond differently. With this understanding of the positions, we will explore some unhealthy behaviours in an intimate relationship. As we have said, there will always be some drama in any human relationship. What is important is to address the unhealthy and unhelpful aspects. While it is fine to have that initial feeling of happiness after receiving their message, it is not a safe place to be if you are relying on them. Your ability to be self-assured or self-soothed is in question. The real danger of relying on others is they are quite likely to let you down without even realising. Without question, there is an issue if you rely on someone else to make you happy or the opposite if you are heavily relied upon.

Seeking external reassurance and love without having internal resources is a recipe for problems. This could mean that you pick the wrong person because there is a belief that you are fulfilled when in a relationship, so you put other needs aside. Maybe you feel lonely or incomplete, which can lead you to start or continue a relationship that is wrong for you.

In these scenarios, having a relationship is what matters rather than checking other important parts of the compatibility. We can find ourselves putting up with negative behaviours.

These limiting beliefs drive the need to be secure with someone else, and unless managed, you are likely to attract someone not necessarily right for you. This is a doubly risky position. There is a high chance that you will be disappointed and then -

crash! If you rely on someone or something else to bring you happiness, you are more than likely not believing in yourself enough. The initial focus must be on the need for self-love and self-acceptance to be successful in a relationship.

The saying goes that you need to love yourself before you can love someone else. If you are not happy within yourself and rely on someone else to make you happy, this is a huge expectation, and the responsibility can be placed on the other person. This can make them run for the hills, or the relationship simply will not work due to the pressure and expectations. The goal is to be happy within, and then a relationship can enhance that happiness, not the other way around.

## People-pleasing (Rescuer)

In an unbalanced relationship, one person may overcompensate to gain approval, which then becomes the norm, and both expect it. For example, someone puts themselves at another's beck and call; whatever they ask for or whenever they make contact, the other person is available. This is not sustainable or healthy and prevents someone from living their own life.

Problems arise when we are running around after someone else too much or not being assertive about our own needs. There is a huge risk that we are not being true to ourselves, and for some, the need to please outweighs anything else. People-pleasers, at their worst, can have low self-esteem and end up being frustrated. They can become indecisive and make choices hoping to keep others happy.

If you are willing to abandon your own work or interests to dedicate yourself to solving the other's problems, there is an issue. It might feel like you are being supportive, but it is actually unhelpful. For some, it is really hard to allow someone to sort things out for themselves.

Another focus for a people-pleaser, is they feel the need to try and prove themselves to others. This also leads to the tendency to become too flexible and completely submissive to others' requests.

In order to make others happy, the people-pleaser will do or say anything to be liked and accepted. There can also be a habit of mind-reading and spending a lot of time and energy trying to think about what the other person wants and needs. This is often misjudged, and actions are not actually what is needed. When we are desperately trying to please others, we are rarely pleasing ourselves.

Not putting yourself first and in the hands of another leads to resentment and unhappiness. There is a risk you are not being true to yourself and having the life you really want.

When we believe that doing whatever the other person wants will keep them happy, problems are ahead. When we make unrealistic sacrifices, then it is likely to lead to unhappiness and unfulfillment. It can be like a vicious circle; we need to feel loved; we adapt ourselves to try and make the person like us and we become unfulfilled. Then we start all over again.

To be successful and happy, the goal is to challenge negative thinking, work out who you really are and then be that person, rather than someone who is driven by their negative fears. When you can be yourself, you will get closer to achieving personal fulfilment and joy.

'Neediness' can stem from feeling a lack (or the wrong kind) of attention, particularly as a child. Maybe growing up where a sibling appeared to have more of the attention, resulting in feeling invisible. The wounds can trigger a desire to cling onto whoever comes into your life. Falling in love can activate these old feelings and some of these behaviours will then play out.

To gain this kind of reassurance, a common behaviour would be the need to talk about every little detail of what is happening in a relationship. There is a constant desire to know how the other person feels, what they are thinking and often a desperation for an immediate response. An example of this could be a multitude of missed calls when apart, as the need for reassurance builds up. This frantic need acts as a mechanism to settle fears or doubts and can create intense relationships. Often there is very little space to be individuals in this kind of situation. In more extreme cases, this 'neediness' can even become abusive and obsessive. It can dominate the relationship and be destructive. This can feel like they are being 'checked up on' although this

is often not seen by the one needing the reassurance.

These behaviours in a relationship create a great deal of pressure and intensity. The fear of rejection or someone being unhappy with you drives this behaviour and again leads you on someone else's path rather than your own.

The 'neediness' drives unnatural expectations, which are difficult to maintain, and each person is left unhappy. The need to be loved or accepted has taken over the fun and natural path of the relationship. When we are looking for love to fulfil a deep-rooted need, then we are heading for a crash.

## Abusive relationships

There are many books and much guidance available about abusive, volatile relationships. In this book, we will simply address the common challenges which are often apparent. These are here because, quite often, a relationship that is unhealthy is not seen as abusive. Some think that if there is no physical violence, it is not abusive, and there are many challenges to getting out of these often very controlling relationships.

This will be a light touch here, although something that is important to acknowledge. The reasons people stay in these types of relationships are no different to relationships that are unfulfilled. As we have mentioned, they are often triggered by a lack of self-belief, self-worth and confidence on behalf of one or both people.

Let us look at common phrases used in unhealthy, abusive relationships and see if we can unpick them a little.

### My partner isn't violent all the time – they love me.

A partner may sometimes be loving and may truly feel sorry for their horrible behaviour. This makes it hard to stay angry and upset with them, so you stay. However, there is a high chance that their violent behaviour will continue. Their behaviour can be incredibly charming and over-compensatory, especially if they are trying to 'win you back' after an episode.

## Things will get better – they didn't mean it.

After a challenging episode, it is common for both parties to try and downplay what happened with excuses, apologies or promises to change. Things might settle down for a bit, but it is often only a matter of time before it happens again. It is very difficult to eradicate abusive behaviour without first taking responsibility and probably seeking professional help.

## It's so confusing – I'm sure it's a one-off.

If you are experiencing abusive, unhealthy behaviours, things can feel really confusing. They will often try to influence your sense of what is real, to make you feel confused or even that you are going crazy.

## Maybe it's *my* fault.

You may begin to think that you are to blame for your partner's abusive behaviour. An abuser may excuse their behaviour by saying something like, 'It wouldn't have happened if you hadn't...' The truth is that no matter what you do, another person's abusive behaviour is never your fault.

## I'm scared of what will happen if I leave them.

It is not unusual to feel afraid of leaving the person who is abusing you. You might feel unsafe or scared of what the person might do to you or themselves. You might also feel that you are not capable of making it on your own. It is important to remember that there are people who can help you every step of the way.

In the next chapter, we will explore some of the challenges around leaving or ending a relationship.

# CHAPTER FIVE

# Leaving or Ending a Relationship

Most of us enter *relationships* with the hope that we will *never* have to *end* them. In most cases, you have shared some *good* times together and there is a part of us that does not want to give up on things.

Seeing a relationship ending as a failure can make it a really difficult time. There may have been too many fallouts and promises that things are going to be different. There is a limit as to how many times this situation can go on for. If the pattern is constantly falling out, particularly when there are big bust-ups, and then many make ups with promises, you are in a tiring and volatile relationship.

At some point, one person needs to step off this roundabout and be honest with themselves and the other person. If we regularly break-up/ make up without professional support, then this revolving door situation is draining and unhealthy. And even with professional help, some couples are just not right for each other. Sometimes people just fall out of love and it is time to end the relationship and move on.

When we get uncomfortable and have a constant feeling of dread, unhappiness, fear or despair within a relationship, this probably means it is time to really think about what is going on.

We have been exploring difficulties in relationships, focusing on why and where these challenges may lie and how each person needs to take responsibility to make necessary changes. Having said that, sometimes, it is just time to be brave and end it.

Ending a relationship can be so difficult. We have invested so much. We have hopes and dreams that it will work out or be different, and yet being totally honest with ourselves, we are miserable and feel like everything has been tried.

Unless there is a huge blow-out that has ended the relationship, finding the right time to end or leave a relationship is never easy. It is often difficult to find the right time to have that difficult conversation.

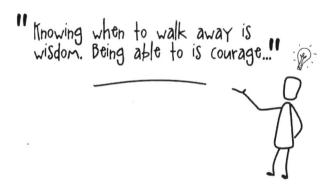

"Knowing when to walk away is wisdom. Being able to is courage..."

There are often social events in the diary which feel either too enormous to go alone or where there is an expectation that you go as a couple. The commitment to the event means the inevitable is delayed, or you may hope that the occasion might help to rekindle the relationship. A holiday or a wedding are classic examples when a couple will try and pull through and go. This is unlikely to work if the issues have not been addressed properly, but if it does, it is usually short-lived.

It is a big deal if you are deciding to leave or end a relationship and there are usually several factors to consider. There is a huge difference depending on where the decision to end lies. Is this a joint decision or only one party? Is this decision coming from one person in the relationship who is unhappy? The chances are if one is unhappy, the other person by default will actually be unhappy too, although this does not always mean that they want to leave or end the relationship. It could be that it has become a place of conflict and there is no option but to end it as the environment has become toxic.

It is very different when only one person has decided they are unhappy. Does that unhappiness come from a lack of fulfilment due to something that is happening or not happening? If one or both parties are not having their needs met, each will often blame the other. This is often not communicated or discussed, and there is a belief that, 'They should know what I need/want.'

In this situation, where no one is communicating well, it is common to stay in drama and conversations remain unhelpful and unproductive.

'Here we are again' is the talk or even self-talk, without any change. We have explored the drama patterns and behaviours already, which gives valuable insight.

Sometimes the only successful outcome is to end a relationship before it becomes too damaging.

## Break-up 'Etiquettes'

There are some 'unwritten rules' in break-ups. Let us quickly explore the key elements.

- Think over what you want and why you want it.
- Take time to consider your feelings and the
- reasons for your decision.
- Think about what you will say and how the other person might react.
- Have good intentions.
- Be honest - but not brutal. We will cover feedback later in the book.
- Say it in person.
- If it helps, confide in someone you trust.

## Rebound

Keep in mind that as humans, we have a huge drive to feel love, be loved and give love. This driver is one of the reasons people tend to 'rebound'. Rebound is when you jump straight into a new relationship as soon as one ends. This can happen in an unhealthy or broken relationship before it has actually ended.

Often people who do this tend to feel that being in a relationship 'makes' them feel better and even whole. It comes back to the 'you complete me' issue we have already explored.

In some cases, the ego and the social self are running the show. Some are driven by the idea that being in a relationship is good for their status, and therefore, a necessity. In these instances, the chances are the person will be unsuitable either way.

Another reason we jump into new relationships is as a 'recovery' strategy. We are so devastated and believe that finding new love will heal our hearts and maybe heal our pride too after someone has ended a relationship. These are all very real scenarios and ones that many do without thought, therefore, out of their awareness.

While this will feel like a solution because we genuinely do feel better, it is not likely to be addressing other hidden challenges. There is no doubt that the language will be, 'I am much happier now', and you will be convincing yourself that the new person is much better. Of course, this may well be true, although the actual chance of this is slim in this situation mainly because you are not moving into this new relationship for the right reason. You have not had any time for reflection and another reality is you will be taking any 'baggage' with you.

This scenario is an indication that something is not right. When we look for a relationship to fix anything emotional, it is a sure sign that our attention is external rather than internal. It is true that having that significant person in your life can reduce loneliness, anxiety and sadness, although, under the wrong conditions, it usually breeds these issues.

With rebound, there has been no time to stop and think about what is happening and, most importantly, what part you play.

It is good to acknowledge that rebounding is something to pay attention to. If appropriate, take time to reflect on yourself in this exercise.

# STEP to CHANGE

Your Experience of Rebound

## Your Experience of Rebound

Take some time to think about this situation for yourself.
Be honest with yourself, and of course, no judgement.

- Have you rebounded before?

- Multiple times?

- Can you identify what was the driver?

- What feelings were you trying to avoid?

- How did it go? Was it successful?

- Can you see a pattern in your relationships?

## Jumping back in

For many of the reasons we have explored in the chapter *Relationships are complex*, there can be a tendency for a couple to keep breaking up and then jumping back in. The situation of breaking up is traumatic and very unhealthy. Whether you are the one doing the finishing or being finished, it is very unsettling and certainly something that should be creating alarm bells.

Something else in the mix is when friends and family are involved in repeated break-ups. They start to make their minds up about the relationship and could feel mistrust. They can hold onto the stories and go into protective mode. This, of course, is what we would expect from our loved ones, although it can cause problems in the future.

The opposite is also true. If we do not talk and share what is happening, the patterns and habits within the relationship stay stuck. It can be that the thoughts are going around in a loop. When we can talk through the challenges, we hear ourselves saying the truth out loud and have to process the situation to put it into words, and there is then another's perspective, which can be invaluable.

Jumping back in because you feel lonely, or have a fear of losing them completely, is a recipe for disaster. In the moment of jumping back in, we may be being driven by our need to be loved and probably are looking through 'rose-tinted glasses' at the relationship rather than taking time to look at the reality.

By recognising these patterns and habits, we are much less likely to repeat them. Once aware of them, we are on our way to making positive changes.

## Taking a break

A break in a relationship occurs when a couple takes time apart before deciding if they want to slay together or break-up for good.

A break can be very healthy in a relationship that is experiencing challenges. It gives an opportunity to explore whether a person feels freer or actually misses their partner. What is important about taking a break is defining clear boundaries. A classic example is Ross and Rachel in *Friends*, who are having a break although there are no boundaries to the break.

A break does not necessarily lead to a break-up, although careful communication is vital before and throughout. There is always a risk that taking the break is interpreted differently by each person. A break can, in fact, strengthen the relationship. Since the reasons for taking a break in a relationship vary, so do the types of breaks that couples can have.

## Divorce and separation

The number one reason why the divorce process is so difficult, no matter how long the marriage was, or how many assets need to be divided, is the simple truth that it is hard to separate the emotions of the marriage and relationship from the business of getting divorced.

The hardest part of a divorce is thinking you have a partner for life. While you are with that partner, you become used to caring about someone else as much, if not more, than you care about yourself, but then one day, it just all disappears.

One of the biggest challenges that many couples or individuals struggle with around divorce or separation is the human driver which worries about what other people will think. This can be at the root of the challenge of ending a relationship, particularly a marriage.

The pain can and does go away, and it does not have to take a year for every five you were married. Getting on the other side of the pain may take a couple of years, although every situation is personal and unique. There is no right or wrong about this. For some, it is a traumatic experience, and for others, it comes as a relief. As ever, there is no judgement here, although ensuring that you come out intact must be your focus.

## The impact of others

We should not underestimate the value we place in other people's opinions of us. As with any views we cast about another, we are not always right, and our thoughts are often more about us than them. Our observations of others often tell us more about us and this can play out in any situation in life, and certainly when there is a relationship break-up.

"Change usually comes out of dissatisfaction..."

There is a skill in being able to understand what others think and how useful this is. Feedback from others can be a blessing or a curse. When we step back and reflect upon another's feedback, we begin to see that it says as much about them as us. This is because we measure each other from where we are.

As an example, think about a relationship that has ended for you and then think about the variety of responses you have received from your friends. Each different response is based on that person's model of the world. This can be why ending a relationship can be confusing, as your friends might see the situation differently. As with any of this understanding, you can often see yourself giving feedback that can only come from your own experience.

The following case study explains this scenario.

Joanne has been married for many years to Terry. They have three children who are all grown up and have left home. Joanne feels lonely in the relationship and does not feel that she and Terry have anything in common anymore. They are both focused on their own work and lives and therefore do very little as a couple. There is no intimacy or an indication of love. She feels like they would be happier if they went their separate ways.

When Joanne tells her group of friends, she has a mixed response. Some friends are supportive, encouraging her to be strong and true to herself. There are also a couple of her friends who are quite critical and say that she should stick at it. They see her in a bad light. Another friend is very fearful and says that she is worried for her going her own way.

Each friend has a different model of the world or lens to see the situation through. This then affects their thoughts. It is good to notice the difference and what situation each friend may be in. The comments are connected to how they feel about relationships and this can cause a negative impact on your decisions.

In this example, can you identify which friends are possibly in a better place and which are more unsettled in their lives?

Sometimes others are simply projecting their own fears or limits onto us.

## Previous break-ups

The main reason people stay broken after break-ups is that they have false beliefs about relationships stored in their subconscious mind. The damage caused by a previous challenge has left false beliefs like: 'I will never find the right one'. 'I am not deserving'. 'It must be me'. 'People will always hurt me'. 'I can't trust anyone'. 'All men are controlling'. Or, 'All women are too emotional'. It can be these kinds of beliefs that stop us from leaving unhealthy relationships.

These unhelpful beliefs can lead to possessiveness, jealousy or other sabotaging behaviours, which will affect any relationship if they are not managed carefully. These behaviours become the focus of the relationship rather than anything that resembles happiness and connection.

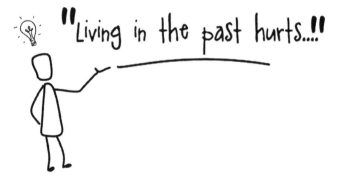

"Living in the past hurts....!"

Many problems arise in relationships simply because old wounds and stories are still around from previous relationships.

The good news is that we can unlearn any negative behaviours and change! When someone feels safe and understands what lies beneath the discomfort, then this kind of situation can start to change. Awareness and acceptance can free a couple from feeling constantly compromised. Then there can be a movement towards a common ground where both feel safe and are able to be themselves.

## After a break-up

When a relationship ends, how many of us have spent time going over what happened and become locked into the details of what was said or done? Or another scenario is focusing, even obsessing on what the other person is doing now. Today's prevalence of social media makes it so tempting to look them up and recreate the discomfort, again and again! This is not healthy to do to yourself and the dangers are the risk of winding yourself up, making up assumptions and a likelihood of feeling alone and isolated by what you think you are seeing. We often imagine that the other person is happier than you at that moment, which may be true because your own behaviours are making you miserable. We are often looking for closure or a justification to settle ourselves. We can obsess to get answers, and often, they are not there. The reasons why relationships end can be many and varied. It would be impossible to explore them all.

We know we are over an ex-partner when we can look at their social media and feel comfortable. We either have no feelings or a feeling of joy. This can be very refreshing. This may mean that enough time has passed, and you are able to handle hearing what they are doing. This usually means that you are feeling good about yourself, which is a great measure.

## Resit class

Many things work out just as they are meant to, yet this is not always a nice journey. We are often so stuck in our heads, overthinking and unable to see the best outcome or why a situation is happening. The trick, and the power, is to work out the messages or learn from these more difficult situations.

When we enter a relationship, which transpires to be wrong for us, the question is: 'What can we learn?'. They must be right for us in some instance or for some period. When we can reflect on what that relationship brought us, we often see something different from just the mismatch. These can be invaluable lessons for us to grow and develop.

Intimate relationships are the most obvious environment for these challenges to occur and, therefore, the best place for the lessons. Another important point is that if you do not pay attention, the lessons will keep repeating until you do. Or you can find yourself a victim of circumstance and you will keep revisiting the resit class! When you are unaware of the hidden pattern, you will continue to be drawn to the wrong kind of person, someone who epitomises your beliefs. For example, if you do not believe you are good enough and you keep meeting people who treat you badly.

If you hear yourself thinking or saying, 'Why does this keep happening to me?', then you are probably attending the resit class. It must be said that in many cases, it takes a lot of work to pull away from these kinds of situations or destructive relationships. The pull to stay with what we know and what we believe we deserve is strong.

These situations create a feeling of being 'stuck'. You are unsure what to do, never mind how to make changes. It can feel like there is no light at the end of the tunnel. Often you do not understand what causes the 'stuck' feeling or why you are behaving the way you are. 'I can't seem to control it'. Or, 'I can't help it'. are common statements. The thinking is autopilot, and the response follows, therefore, a pattern.

When we can spot our patterns, we are well on our way to shifting them and freeing ourselves, so we are less likely to repeat the same situation. When we feel overwhelmed by negative emotions, we often put this down to the other person's behaviour. When we can understand both our responses and the other's, we can start to have real insights into our patterns in relationships.

Our self-limiting or negative beliefs cause us to distort and negatively interpret situations. Whatever you believe about yourself affects you in most, if not all, situations. For example, if you believe you do not deserve to be treated well, then you are likely to attract people who treat you poorly and put you down. Your belief of yourself is then validated. This kind of person is clearly not a positive influence in your life, although the secret message is more about you than them. The feedback for you and the reason you attracted them into your life was for you to see these often-hidden beliefs and work towards changing them.

## Ending it

Our culture can have a romantic ideal about relationships. In so many movies with romance at the centre, there is bound to be a desperate and needy character who treats themselves badly for the sake of being in love with someone.

The truth is our view of what a successful relationship should be is pretty confusing. If a relationship ends, we can view it as a failure, regardless of the emotional or practical circumstances present in the person's life. The reason for the relationship ending could be a really positive step, yet we seem to see it as a bad thing.

Being willing to end an unhealthy relationship shows strength, self-worth, self-love and confidence. These are everything that most people are looking for and ending a broken relationship actually gives you these, although this is usually lost in the discomfort.

It is perfectly ok to call it quits on a relationship that feels unfair or is not working for you. What we need to pay attention to is what we can learn so that we are not a victim of the resit class with the next relationship.

## Letting go of someone you love

After a difficult break-up, there are some simple do's for yourself:

- avoid contact
- own what you are feeling
- stay away from fantasising
- practise forgiveness, self and others
- understand the grieving process. It is a loss
- reach out for support
- take all the time you need
- prioritise your own needs
- stop checking their social media
- resist temptation to start a new relationship

## Catalyst for change

When we have been able to look at a relationship through a different lens and identify which behaviours belong to which partner, then we can start to see the real root of both the problems and the solutions. A relationship, or the partners in the relationship, can support each other to make the greatest changes. This could mean together or, in some instances, is better separately.

We eventually realise that an intimate relationship is like a mirror. Our partner has an uncanny ability to reflect back to us the parts of ourselves that need the most healing. If we understand this, we can learn to use the conflict in our relationship as a catalyst for growth.

We can stop the blame and anger. Instead, we feel immense gratitude when we find yet another old wound in need of healing. This is how we grow as individuals or together if the relationship can manage the healing. In these situations, during the process, we create great connection and intimacy.

In an intimate relationship, we are like two rough pieces of sandpaper, constantly rubbing up against each other. Over time, if we use this process to our benefit, we become smoother. Then, our relationship reflects back to us this smoother, gentler, happier version of ourselves.

Sometimes when couples break-up, some friends or acquaintances find themselves thinking: 'I would never have expected them to split'. Or, 'They appeared to have a good relationship'. This can do one of two things; it can help you refocus on your relationship and how you can improve it, or it could make you wobble, as you can now feel very threatened.

## Show strength

If we are courageous enough to end an unhealthy relationship, knowing many of the pitfalls we have explored in this chapter, we know now we need to focus our attention on ourselves. We will have started to let go of old anger, stopped talking about feeling unappreciated and have begun to look forward to a new future. In this vein, we need to think about prioritising our own needs for ourselves.

Before we move on, regardless of our circumstances – single, married, dating, co-habiting – we need to think about what is important to us.

Prioritise self:

- fitness
- look after yourself – self-care
- make your own plans
- the belief you are enough
- maintain friendships and ultimately, be willing to walk away.

In the next chapter, we will bring this all together and think about what makes up a healthy relationship.

# CHAPTER SIX

# Healthy Relationships

A happy, healthy relationship is created with many different ingredients. A fundamental piece is that both people actually want to be together. As relationships can be a difficult path to navigate, this is vital. It does sound mad saying that, it is certainly not a given.

In this chapter, we will explore the key ingredients to supporting a relationship to be a success. We have identified how challenges and complexities can affect a relationship. Each person's 'baggage' of life, past relationships and experiences need to be considered as they can make a difference to its success.

Everyone deserves to be in a relationship that is fulfilling in a mutual way, and the effort is reciprocated. A healthy relationship means each person can be themselves. It is important to have two individuals in a relationship who are happy within and with themselves, rather than relying heavily on the relationship to bring happiness. Of course, we gain lots when we are in a relationship, although it is not healthy to have this as the driver. It is also vital to remember that no one is a possession. A healthy relationship gives the gift of allowing each other to flourish and grow. There is nothing better than feeling like you are each other's cheerleader, and that you feel you can rely on one another. Every couple achieves their own compromise, and this is unique to them.

There are many words that spring to mind that fit with a healthy relationship – adapting, flexing, accepting, forgiving...although these are not always freely available to us, and we need to be conscious about doing them. We will explore these and much more throughout this chapter.

## Change is within you

Relationships help us grow and evolve. They are for us to be conscious of who we really are. Remember that no one can cover all our needs or fill the emptiness we feel inside. We need to find the someone inside of us to complete us, instead of hoping that the someone else will save us.

We need to constantly highlight that self-love and belief make the biggest difference to a successful relationship. To be able to fulfil all the aspects in this chapter, we must pay close attention to ourselves and how we view ourselves, as much as watching the relationship itself.

## Self-love – Be yourself

A natural goal for all of us is to be happy in life. When we take full responsibility for ourselves, then we have the control and the right ingredients to actually make that happen. When you are free to decide your own path and focus on what you really want and deserve, then momentum is there. This, of course, needs to be agreed within the boundaries of the relationship.

The key is to love your partner, although not sacrifice yourself so much that you build up frustration and resentment.

I love you, but I do not need you.

## Cornerstones

There are so many components to what would make up a healthy relationship. There are some key features that create a solid foundation. In this section, we will refer to them as cornerstones. It is hard to decide what is a cornerstone, and bear in mind that each person will interpret the ones that are the most important to them.

## Respect

Respect is one of the key cornerstone of any healthy relationship. Respect means that you recognise that your partner is a whole person and not just a way to get something you want. It means that you know your partner has different experiences and opinions from you, and that is ok. Someone respecting your opinion as you would respect theirs. And the willingness to do that allows us to establish the necessary boundaries to help ourselves and our partner grow together.

Receiving respect from others is important because it helps us to feel safe and to express ourselves. Respect means accepting somebody for who they are, even when they have a different viewpoint or could disagree with you. Respect in your relationships builds feelings of trust, safety, and wellbeing.

It is also important to be able to say what is ok for you and how something makes you feel, with no fear of any repercussions.

So, for example, if you say to your partner, 'I did not like it when you laughed at me because of my morning hair', they will respond more sensitively and appropriately. 'I did not mean to upset you', would be far more respectful than a statement like, 'Can't you take a joke?'. The latter can make you feel like you are super sensitive.

Part of a healthy relationship is being interested in each other's lives, asking how each is doing, asking about little things, being interested in big things in their life and taking the time to get to know them even better.

## Trust

Trust is another cornerstone of any relationship. Without it, two people cannot be comfortable with each other and the relationship will lack stability. It is trust that allows us to navigate the uncertain and complex world we live in today. Trust is something that is earned, and in relationships, this can be achieved in different ways. Most often through actions and also behaviours. Trust grows the sense of security that allows both parties to expose themselves fully without any judgements or fears. Trust builds slowly as we learn about our partner and they become predictable to us.

Trust usually precedes love; we can only truly love someone that we can trust.

Cheating is not a mistake you make when you truly love someone.

## Honesty

Honesty is the foundation for trust in a relationship, and trust is necessary for a relationship to function and thrive. A common misconception is that being honest is not telling lies, although it is so much more than that. Being honest means being your true self around your partner, never hiding who you are, what you think, or how you feel. Being honest with your partner also facilitates healthy communication, which is also necessary for a functional relationship.

Couples need to be able to talk to each other openly and be real; that is what true connection is all about. That commitment to being honest also means that both people will be proactive about addressing any tension, conflicts, or issues in the relationship, bringing them up to their partner for discussion.

Honesty in a relationship also means telling your partner the truth and being totally open with them, both for the big things and the little things.

There are many challenges to this which link back to some of the difficulties around self-belief, having a voice, being worried about how someone will react and jealousy.

Sometimes couples can get a little wrapped up in trying to make sure they know absolutely everything about each other. Clearly, there are times when sharing too much could be hurting your independence and sense of self. It is essential to understand the difference between secrets and privacy.

## Honesty versus privacy

Think of it this way: privacy is a boundary around one's own thoughts, ideas, and past experiences that do not directly involve one's partner. A secret is something that is misleading in some way and intentionally kept hidden from them for fear of judgement or reprisal.

Partners do not need to tell each other absolutely everything to be considered honest. But they do need to be transparent about information that directly affects each other's well-being. A good rule of thumb is that if you are actively avoiding telling your partner something because you are worried about their reaction, you are keeping a secret and intentionally being dishonest. And if your partner asks you something directly, you do need to tell the truth. If not, and you miss information out, then there needs to be a consideration as to whether this is healthy. As trust can sit sensitively at the heart of honesty, it is something that can cause a lot of issues.

Some think that they are protecting a partner by not being honest about something that they have decided will not be received well or misunderstood. This approach is proven to be damaging as most people admit that they would rather know than have something going on behind their back.

A good measure of balancing honesty and privacy is to consider if you would like it done to you. To ask yourself, 'How would I feel if there was something happening without my knowing?', usually gives you a foundation. The trick is to consider how to discuss it rather than avoid it. It usually comes back in a negative way, and then the risk is it blows up into a much bigger situation than the original scenario.

## Self-exposure

We form more intimate connections with people with whom we disclose important information about ourselves. Indeed, self-disclosure is a characteristic of healthy intimate relationships, as long as the information disclosed is consistent with our own views. Self-exposure opens the door to profound love, connection and fulfilment.

## Reliability

It is important to think of the factors that help build up trust and one of them is reliability. Being reliable builds trust – it is vital for a partner to know that they can count on you to keep your word, be there when you say you will, and do what you say you will do.

An example is when you get invited to a wedding and you automatically know that you can accept on behalf of you both, with no doubt. You feel 100 percent sure.

## Flexibility

Being flexible is a conscious decision, and it is something to master, as unconsciously, we can stick rigidly to our own ideas. Having this in a relationship has many benefits. Often, individuals choose the path of resistance and refusal to change because they equate being flexible as giving in or as a weakness.

Reciprocity is the give and take in relationships. We contribute to relationships, but we expect to receive benefits as well. That is, we want our relationships to be a two-way street, and trust comes when we can rely on this to happen.

Balanced relationships should be closer to 50/50 when it comes to give and take. Give and take is a mechanism inherent to all personal relationships – you cannot expect to receive something if you do not freely give. Once the balance between give and take is broken, difficulties arise, and partners feel they are not getting as much from their relationship.

In a healthy relationship, different quirks and habits will feel tolerable and are therefore tolerated. They are not a deal-breaker. In a long-term relationship, it is important to overlook some little habits, partly to keep the peace, though mainly making allowances for differences in each other. This does need to be reciprocated and not one-sided. When this tolerance is lacking, it often means there is a deeper-rooted problem and criticism can be a noted behaviour. When one is annoyed with the other's habits, often in everything they do, this is a time to be honest.

Without this reflection, it is frustrating as these situations will keep playing out and generally cause hurt, upset, confusion, or annoyance. As with any behaviours, once we are aware it is happening, we are on our way to an alternative.

## Appreciation

Appreciation is one of the keys to building healthy relationships and can allow the great potential to flourish.

When we appreciate each other, we connect to our loving selves and we expand and grow. We evolve in our relationships, and we take more responsibility for the way we are with others. We want to share and not hide parts of ourselves, to let the other see just how much we can shine, and it feels great!

Whether you are taking each other for granted, just coasting along or want to take your relationships to a whole new level, it is vital to take the time to express appreciation. This can make a big difference in building a healthy relationship. It can bring you back to the essence of why you are with each other in the first place ... and that is love.

An area that can cause challenges is when there is a mismatch around effort, which leads to a lack of appreciation. For example, one may spend a long time cooking a lovely meal for their partner, but they have made a bit of a mess in the kitchen. The partner comes home and cannot see the effort or appreciate the meal because the mess causes them stress. The appreciation is lost through each other's differences.

## Acceptance

Acceptance can be an overused statement. We often say that we accept situations or people and yet complain bitterly, without really stopping to notice that we do this.

In relationships, we often find ourselves focusing on each other's faults and mistakes rather than the unique qualities we all bring.

It is, generally, normal to have reacted to something difficult. What is not helpful is holding onto that reaction. When we accept a situation or our behaviour at the time or soon afterwards, we will allow ourselves to move forward and let go of any negativity. Quite commonly we find ourselves frustrated with the situation and/or ourselves, which is unhelpful.

By accepting a situation, we can settle ourselves. This must be done carefully as our minds will be focused on the feelings that came with the situation. Its job is to protect you, so it will remind you of the feeling by way of an alarm system. A partner has done something you were unhappy with; if you hold on to that, then you will constantly feel annoyed or upset. We must be quite conscious about accepting that something happened in a certain way and understand that the other person is likely to have thought their behaviour was right.

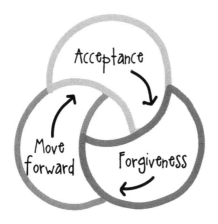

This becomes the challenge with relationships because each individual is interpreting the situation through their lens. Just to be clear, as we explored in an earlier chapter, we are not talking about accepting unacceptable behaviours.

As with anything, the real challenge is accepting yourself, your flaws, what has happened and also the flaws of your partner. Acceptance is probably one of the most powerful approaches available to us.

## Accepting and celebrating differences

It is normal and can be fairly common to wish that others were different, just like it is normal to wish that you were different. For example, you might wish you were thinner, richer or wiser.

Accepting people does not itself mean agreeing with them, waiving your own rights, or downplaying their impact upon you. You can still take appropriate action to protect or support yourself or others. Or you can simply let people be. Either way, you accept the reality of the other person. You may not like it, you may not prefer it, you may feel sad or angry about it, but at a deeper level, you are at peace with it. In most situations, the shift to acceptance will help things get better.

Consider how you have got involved and struggled to accept someone as they are. We can notice a range of behaviours like judgement, pushiness, irritability and narrow mindedness. The task is to notice that firstly you are in this struggle with them and become open to easing your thinking. This creates relief and peace:

- Every person has flaws and imperfections.
- You cannot ever *force* a person to change.
- Therefore, you must be with somebody who has flaws you can live with or even appreciate.
- Is it something my partner can change?

It may be our perfections that attract one another in the first place. But it is our imperfections that decide whether or not we stay together.

The most accurate metric for your love of somebody is how you feel about their flaws. If you accept them and even adore some of their shortcomings - her obsessive cleanliness, his awkward social tics - and they can accept and even adore some of your shortcomings, this is a sign of a healthy relationship.

In the movie, *Bridget Jones*, Mark Darcy says to Bridget, "I like you just the way you are." This is a perfect example of acceptance and understanding of her imperfections.

Consider how much you like it when you feel that another person accepts you completely. It is a beautiful gift — and we can give this gift to others when we accept them. Imagine how it might improve your relationship with someone if that person felt you accepted him or her fully. Acceptance is a gift that keeps on giving.

The next exercise helps you to consider your own behaviours around accepting others.

# STEP to CHANGE

## Accepting Others

## Accepting Others

Take some time to think about this for yourself.

In what ways do you wish that people were different?

Think about your relationship.

Who do you need to accept?

If you like, be more specific, naming aspects of this person that particularly bother you, such as: "I accept that you ... snore ... leave your clothes on the floor ... are still angry with me."

I accept ............................... happened,
and I am willing to let go of ..........................

..................................................

I accept ............................... happened,
and I am willing to let go of ..........................

..................................................

I accept ............................... happened,
and I am willing to let go of ..........................

..................................................

If you have done this on a separate piece of paper, you
can destroy the paper - rip it up or burn it (carefully!)
Now think of all the parts of yourself you find difficult
to accept.

Either say the following each day or even while you
look in the mirror.

I accept ............................... about myself

I accept ............................... about myself

I accept ............................... about myself

## What is acceptable and what is not

In some situations, what is considered acceptable and unacceptable has so many parameters, and it can be this that causes conflict. Being able to separate what is acceptable or not can be one of the most difficult parts of a relationship. Who is right? Is someone wrong? If a behaviour is causing a difficulty, it needs to be addressed. Although remembering that the growth will lie with both parties identifying their part rather than just blaming.

It is important to say here that when we accept a situation, this does not mean that we need to like it or agree with it. It means to be able to move on, we need to accept what has happened. Some people say that acceptance makes us vulnerable and like a 'doormat'. It is actually the opposite as you take back the power. By accepting what has happened and dealing with your part in it, then you can be free from mental and emotional blockages.

Quite often, our own behaviour, and that of others, is negative and sometimes clearly unacceptable. This still is not healthy to hold on to. By letting go, we can become more rational and reasonable – and peaceful. We can choose to accept the other person's ways as just that, bearing in mind no one is perfect. This allows us to move on. Practising and mastering acceptance shifts you into accepting yourself fully as the person you are.

Real self-acceptance comes from accepting the things you like about yourself and the things you do not. It comes from allowing yourself to experience thoughts and feelings without denial, self-punishment or rejection. By learning to accept yourself, your attention can work on the self-limiting beliefs that hold you back rather than self-punishment.

## Forgiveness

Forgiveness is not easy and can often be more painful than the initial hurt itself. As with acceptance, forgiveness does not mean that we are excusing someone else's or our own poor behaviour. When we let go of the hurtful emotions associated with memories of the past, we become peaceful and claim back our power to cope in the future. By holding on, we are draining ourselves and will stay weakened. By freeing ourselves, we become stronger and more resilient. Forgiveness can be described as liberating and this comes from both forgiving others and self.

Forgiving those involved in old stories of a past relationship or situation helps us grow and focus on new things in the future. When we think of all the things that went wrong and sit in blame, it brings negativity and risks the likelihood of the same behaviours reoccurring.

Self-forgiveness is like reclaiming our freedom from the past and this can often be harder work than forgiving others. It is the one form of forgiveness that most people neglect. Through being curious and self-reflective, we find ourselves in a state of forgiveness. We are the only ones who can separate ourselves from other people's drama.

Learning to forgive ourselves and others is no mean feat. It takes determination and commitment. It also takes time, and you also may need to repeat it several times. This needs to be a conscious action.

This next exercise is powerful and needs to be repeated regularly. Take time and write down your answers. Seeing them visually strengthens the power and helps with the repetitive nature of changing the thinking habits of the mind.

Recall anyone in your life who you hold a negative emotion or thought about. Then write and read out the answers to these statements.

Repeat and repeat until you feel a sense of relief.

# STEP to CHANGE

Forgiveness

## Forgiveness

Take a moment to think about your own situation.

### Forgiveness of Others

The person I need to forgive is .....................................................
and I forgive you for ...................................................................


The person I need to forgive is .....................................................
and I forgive you for ...................................................................


The person I need to forgive is .....................................................
and I forgive you for ...................................................................


Do this time and time again.

## Forgiveness of Self

Now turn the exercise onto yourself, and think about all the things that you blame yourself for and say:

I truly forgive myself for ......................................................................

I truly forgive myself for ......................................................................

I truly forgive myself for ......................................................................

Again, repeat and repeat until you feel a sense of relief.

## Space

Another positive and yet often missed aspect of a healthy relationship is having some time apart. This is important for each person and the relationship as a whole. Having time apart is extremely healthy and keeps a relationship fresh. It encourages each person to maintain their own sense of identity while still being a couple, and it fosters independence and strength rather than neediness.

Space in a relationship is an essential requirement of every partner aspiring to have a happy life together. Having your partner by your side comes with a great feeling of comfort but understanding why you need some space to yourself is vital and key to a great relationship.

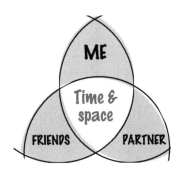

Space in a relationship does not affect your happy moments together. It benefits both individuals involved in the relationship, as it prevents the bond from falling apart. A lot of people complain that they have lost their identity in their relationship because they do not know who they are without their partner, which is why space is important. If you are considering reconnecting with your true self, then you should take space seriously.

Having some 'alone time' does not mean your relationship is struggling. For some, they see the need for space as a sign that the relationship is at breaking point, yet it can keep your relationship from getting to that point.

It is essential that you use this time to yourself wisely. Being able to spend some time on personal development shows you care for yourself and the relationship. This time helps to increase your self-confidence and happiness, which you then take back into the relationship. This supports you being happy for your partner in their life, successes and achievements. This can clearly be done within the relationship, although often, our truths need to have space to be explored.

There were people in your life before you met your partner: friends, family or colleagues, and saving time for these connections is also critical. Spending time with people that genuinely care about you outside your relationship provides a solid foundation. It is also good to expand your network to accommodate new people.

Having some separate friends, taking an occasional trip somewhere by yourself, or having a hobby you enjoy without your partner are all important aspects of each person maintaining their own independence and identity. It also helps us to remember who we are and what attracted us to our partner in the first place.

Your world should not revolve around your partner only. Spending quality time with other people in your life strengthens the relationship you have with them. If you argue or fight in the future, these are people you can rely on for help.

"Don't abandon your friends..."

It is important to occasionally get some distance from your partner, assert your independence, maintain some hobbies or interests that are yours alone.

## Shared interests

While it is great to enjoy shared interests and hobbies, it does not work for everyone. In new relationships, you often want to spend lots of time together and can become interested in each other's passions. It is, however, not a condition to the relationship lasting if you have a lack of shared interests. The trick here is to be interested and encouraging if there are no shared hobbies. The point being, relationships are complex and unique formulas, not a one-size-fits-all template.

## A different perspective

In a relationship, you cannot agree on every decision made. Being with your partner 24/7 can lead to unnecessary fights and arguments. However, some time out can help keep respect and composure in order to avoid the little arguments that can get blown out of proportion.

When there is tension in a relationship, having time apart can make positive changes and it helps to give a different perspective. We can get a new view alone, although there is often more power in sharing with someone you trust. Often hearing yourself say things out loud to a friend can help on its own. If you have thoughts flying around in your head, saying them to someone else means that you have to form sentences, so you are making more sense for yourself.

As we have said, being safe and sharing your experiences with a trusted friend outside the relationship gives us clarity and/or reassurance. It is worth considering who you confide in when times are difficult. Ensure it is someone you trust and will be helpful rather than someone who may take you down the wrong path. Talking your challenges through can give a renewed view of the relationship and this can act as a strong vehicle to getting the right kind of changes.

Sometimes they say that a problem shared is a problem halved. Quite often, when you listen to another's challenges, it indirectly helps you. It can help simply as a reminder that you are not alone, and others have difficulties too or may be experiencing something similar. When you hear your friend say, 'I could respond like that too', then you instantly feel more settled. Also, by hearing someone else work out what they need, you are able to take strength or ideas from this. It is not to be underestimated how powerful giving another person your time can be.

## Values aligned and understood

We have already talked about what values are, their power and how we need to ensure that we are fulfilling them in life.

Once we have established our own individual values around a relationship, it is an interesting exercise to ensure that each person in the relationship understands each other's values. It then becomes a shared experience rather than there being doubt or confusion about where each one is coming from.

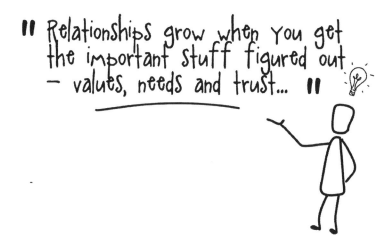

" Relationships grow when you get the important stuff figured out — values, needs and trust... "

A couple can explore their values together in a relationship. It is good to understand each other's values, the shared values, but critically it is important to ensure that they are aligned. By aligned we mean having a perception and understanding of these values. For example, love which is subjective can be interpreted differently and even though it can be a shared value, it presents itself differently for each person. As we have said, misunderstandings can negatively affect a relationship which can lead to blame. Knowing what values actually mean to each other can be a game changer.

# Understanding expectations

In a healthy relationship, people have high expectations for how they want to be treated. They expect to be treated with kindness, love, affection and respect. They do not tolerate emotional or physical abuse. They expect their partner to be loyal.

Being in a healthy relationship means you are getting your needs met by a person you love and trust. The opposite to this is when expectations can destroy a relationship. When you expect your partner to do things that you have not communicated to them, or have unreasonable expectations, then problems arise. How can they possibly do this? They are your partner, not a mind reader.

In general, as humans, we often expect others to think and behave as we would. It comes as a great shock when someone does something different and against what we had expected. The fact that you expected something could leave you in trouble. This can then cause challenges and arguments.

We need to spend time being clear on our expectations and keep them alive and up to date. We often do this at the beginning and then seem to forget further into the relationship.

Let us reflect on your own expectations in the next exercise. You are encouraged to think about yourself, your partner and then the relationship.

# STEP to CHANGE

## Expectations

## Expectations

Take some time to think about what expectations you put on yourself, your partner and your relationship.

What do you expect of yourself?

Is this reasonable?

What do you expect of your partner?

Is this reasonable?

What do you expect from your relationship?

Is this reasonable?

## Complain without blame

The antidote for criticism is to complain without blame by using a soft or gentle start-up. Avoid saying "you" which can indicate blame. Instead, talk about your feelings using "I" statements and express what you need in a positive way.

Have a think about these questions for yourself.

- How can you manage not to hurt each other or your relationship when you have a row?
- How can you learn from the conflict?

We have explored the positions on the drama triangle. This helps us understand what is happening in a time of conflict, although the real task is being able to act without blame.

## Focus on the issues at hand

Conflict in relationships often come as the original issue gets lost. Extra details, bringing up past experiences and emotions, move the couple away from the initial disagreement.

When we are able to speak openly about an issue at the time, we are more likely to remain rational. If issues are left unresolved or get added to other challenges, this usually means the focus has been lost.

## Take responsibility

We have explored the negative side of taking unnecessary responsibility in a relationship. The positive side is when we can have open communication about feelings. Each person is willing to admit that we can grow from the hard parts of the relationship. When both partners learn to take responsibility for their own behaviours and hold themselves accountable for their actions, then we see movement. It is important to remember that each person in a relationship has to take their own responsibility, has an opportunity to grow and develop, which all contribute to a healthy relationship. Each person has to be willing and open to this.

## Letting some conflicts go unresolved

There are two ways to let go of conflict. There is 'pretend' letting go. This is when one or both say they will move on and shrug something off, though this does not happen. Instead, you allow it to eat away at you or influence your future interactions in the relationship. 'Pretend' letting go is just another form of avoidance.

Genuine letting go is when you decide to move on and hold yourself to your commitment. It is based on self-awareness and commitment to act on your decision.

# Feedback

Feedback from others and towards others can, and is, a huge subject. In fact, whole books are written just on this. The important part about feedback is to be able to separate the really unhelpful 'useless' feedback from real feedback, which is useful. The prime place for useless feedback is when someone is in drama. It is also interesting to note that some unhelpful comments can reflect the speaker and their own issues.

A simple example could be a throw-away comment like, 'You are overweight'. This could be changed into something like, 'Shall we shop for healthy options for us both?'. This is supportive and helpful.

## Dismiss useless feedback

Fortunately, you can tell these things apart because they feel very different. Useless feedback is either very blunt, non-specific, vague or has no action implication. It demotivates, locking us in confusion and shame. This is the kind that we need to dismiss and yet often has the greater impact.

On the other hand, useful feedback is specific and focused. As we have said previously, some feedback can sting initially and be uncomfortable though it can be our greatest gift. This can lead to growth and development. These can be like lightbulb moments once they have been accepted and processed.

Another example is, 'No one could ever love you', is useless feedback. The opposite could be, 'You project a lot of hostility, and it scares people'. This gives you information that you need to make healthy changes. It is safe to assume that useless feedback is coming from people who are themselves shame-bound and blind. The best thing to do with it is dismiss it and focus on the information your gut tells you, which is likely to be valuable.

** Feedback needs to make
   sense to the receiver... **

Deliberately, methodically eliminating your blind spots simply intensifies the natural process we all endure as life teaches us its rough-and-tumble lessons. If you undertake this accelerated journey, you will learn much more in much less time (albeit with a few more scrapes and bruises) and achieve a deeper level of self-knowledge than you otherwise would have.

Just observing the truth about yourself without judgement will begin to change you.

## Planning the future

It is healthy to talk about the future and for both parties in the relationship to be excited. It is important to say, though, that difficulties can arise, even in this area. It would seem that the future can only be positive, although people project differently into the future. Some absolutely love to plan, love to know what is coming up and are comfortable to forward plan well into the future. This is not true for everyone, though. Some people more naturally focus and think day by day and find planning both unnecessary and, in some instances, even scary.

With any of these situations, the key is to be aware of the differences and work together.

Many couples work really well having some plans for the future, although watch out when this causes unnecessary conflict. There is a risk that someone not wanting to plan for the future can create insecurities about commitment, and yet it could be 'just' how each individual processes the future. Understanding this can be relationship changing.

# STEP to CHANGE

## Planning Ahead

# Planning Ahead

Now have a think about yourself.

Do you like to plan ahead for the future?

How far? When does it get uncomfortable?

Do you prefer spontaneity or immediate plans?

If you are in a relationship, consider these questions for your partner.

We have been looking at some key elements to a healthy relationship. By taking the time to consider that everyone may be different in their understanding and interpretation, we then start to see our relationships through a different lens.

Just by considering that the conflict could be a difference rather than a personal attack, we can start making more sense of our relationship and each person in it.

In the following short chapter, we will look a little further into types of communication, which can enhance a relationship.

We know now that everything is a form of communication, although some specific information will give a greater chance of improving it.

# CHAPTER SEVEN

# Communication Styles

# Communication starts with you

We have established that human communication and relationships are some of the most complex things in life. As incredible as we are, we are limited in our ability to truly understand others: why they do the things they do, why they say the things they say and what they actually mean.

It can all feel like a mystery because we all process and interpret everything differently. The problem is we are often focused on other people and trying to understand them. We usually do this without understanding ourselves first, and when we are unsure how our own minds work, why do we try to decipher someone else's?

It does help to remember that everyone is not thinking and feeling the same as you. Knowing this helps you to adjust your expectations.

It is vital to remember that each of us is unique and that each person's 'map of their reality' is personal, intimate, and incomparable to anyone else's.

In order to understand our own world, we attempt to apply meaning and our own interpretation to other people's actions, behaviours and communications. We can get into 'sticky' territory when we expect others to behave the same as us. We will all have people that are more like us than others, although our minds work differently based on the information and interpretations of experiences. We never truly know what is going on in someone else's mind and how they view the world.

The trouble starts when we try to second guess what is going on for someone else. Mind reading and making assumptions are prevalent and we rarely stop to think about how unique styles of communication are.

In this chapter, we will explore some of the differences that may play out in our communication. With an understanding, we can make changes in how we communicate and what we expect from others. We will also be having a light look at some of the differences between how men and women communicate.

## Communicating skills

This is an interesting topic, and when it is understood, it can help explain many challenges in our conversations, particularly within intimate relationships.

So often, arguments with partners can be far more heated than they need to be, and this is down to different unconscious communication styles. It is like we are on different radio frequencies or even speaking a foreign language.

There are two styles for speaking and two styles for listening, and it is invaluable to understand the differences. Everyone generally falls into one category, although this is not set in stone. We can all listen and speak in either style at different times, although generally, we each have a tendency towards one.

When someone does not understand what you are saying, then arguments and misunderstandings occur. The response can be that people feel unheard, undervalued, unloved, uncared for, when often it is just a simple difference in communication styles.

When you understand these two different styles, then we can be flexible, learn to talk or listen to support a better conversation. Sometimes we might need to change how we say something or appreciate what the other is saying.

Let us look at the two types first and then explore how this can affect a relationship.

## Literal versus inferential

We have people who have a greater tendency to be a literal speaker who, as hinted in the name, will speak literally and specifically about what they mean. 'Please get me a glass of water', is a literal request. Then on the opposite side of the scale, there is an inferential speaker. They will weave around a topic hoping the other person will guess or work out what they are saying. 'Oh, I am so thirsty', is an inferential request. They are not asking clearly for what they want, although they often expect someone to hear their 'request'.

Can you see the difference?

Few of us are 100 percent literal or inferential but sit somewhere in between. One thing to remember, there is no right or wrong and no 'better' way to be.

Generally speaking, and this is a sweeping statement, men can be more literal speakers, and often, women are more likely to speak inferentially.

Just to complicate the situation, we also have the same two different styles for listening. Some listen literally, while others listen inferentially.

Can you see the challenge when this is not understood?

A person who listens literally can take an instruction or information to an unnecessary place. On the other side, someone who listens inferentially will hear hints from conversations and decide that there is an instruction. They are more likely to take action even when this is not needed.

This can create a lot of miscommunication in relationships where one partner will give clues and hints like, 'Oh, it would be so nice if we went on a holiday', and the other partner is listening and thinking, 'Why do you keep talking about this?'. They are not sure what is being said, as they do not hear the hidden request. On the other hand, the inferential speaker thinks that they are being clear, which then becomes another issue.

Someone who hears inferentially can hear the request, can read between the lines and hears, 'They must mean that they want to go on holiday, let us book one!'.

An inferential speaker and listener may think that the literal person is harsh and almost rude. This can cause challenges, as you can imagine.

These communication styles can cause challenges in relationships, particularly between men and women. A man might listen literally, so they respond to specific, clear, tangible instructions and do not understand references, hints and subtle cues. At the same time, a woman may think they are giving instructions through hints and gets frustrated when their partner does not respond.

These styles can be and should be used in a different context. For example, when speaking to children, you might be more literal than when speaking to your partner or family member.

The most important aspect here is to be aware of the differences, as understanding them can be a game changer in relationships.

Take some time now to think about your own communication styles and see if they are serving you.

# STEP to CHANGE

## Your Communication Style

## Your Communication Style

Reflect on your communication style. As ever, no judgement with this exercise.

Do you tend to be a literal listener?

or inferential listener?

Do you tend to be a literal speaker?

or inferential speaker?

Can you see how this causes challenges?

Notice how you speak to different people.

Notice how other people in your life communicate when they are speaking and then listening?

Could you stretch your communication style to be able to use the opposite style?

Can you be clearer with instructions?

Can you ask your partner, 'Please tell me specifically what you want?'

Can you clarify with the other person,
'I think you mean this ......... Is that right?'

## Feeling heard

Now we have explored two different styles of speaking and listening, it is important to link this with active listening and feeling heard. It is fairly common to hear people say that they do not feel heard or listened to.

There is probably nothing better than being heard and also understood. Active listening is a skill and one that most people are not great at doing. We are often listening to respond rather than listening to understand. This means we are usually processing the response in our own heads rather than truly listening.

We, therefore, have to make an active choice to listen. We need to be conscious and set a goal to listen. Often eye-contact and paying attention to the other person can help. The natural response is to do the opposite, which can cause difficulties.

Evidence that active listening is happening is allowing each person to finish what they are saying before the other speaks. Over talking and interrupting can become a habit and is often at the root of not feeling heard and understood. It sounds like a simple suggestion but minimising distractions such as mobiles creates the right environment for a healthy conversation. Once an intention to listen has been set, there is also a benefit in having an agreement to seek a resolution and move in the right direction. It is also worth clarifying what has been agreed and this will flush out any misinterpretations. Remember that each person is making their own interpretations.

## Improving communication

Once you have established how you speak and listen, you can use this information when you feel like you are being misunderstood.

You can reflect on this exercise and just ask yourself, 'Am I speaking literally or inferentially? And could the other person be listening or speaking literally or inferentially?'. Then you can use your communication to clarify what is going on and create harmony. When you see it through this lens, you can see that some misunderstandings really are unnecessary.

Some people feel very comfortable being literal and will not feel comfortable being inferential. Some people will be the opposite – very comfortable inferring things but not very comfortable being literal.

With any of these differences, it is important to remember that we are not judging anyone else or ourselves. It is merely to improve our communications and have some flexibility to create peace. It makes sense.

## Male and female differences

This topic is also huge, and this book is certainly not a place to focus too deeply on the differences between male and female. However, it is worth noting a few other pointers to assist with challenges.

It is probably fair to say, with a smile on our face, that men and women are different species and have many differences when it comes to how we process. It is good to cover this here as sometimes the knowledge can help adjust expectations. We spend time thinking, hoping and believing that someone, anyone, will respond just as we expect them to. This is particularly apparent when it comes to people in close relationships.

Misunderstandings arise between men and women when they fail to realise that their partner does not react as they would react. This is actually true for anyone in any situation, as often we expect someone to react as we would, which does cause challenges.

However, coming back to intimate relationships, this often plays out even more due to the close nature of the relationship.

In general, men prefer to be focused, logical and independent in their problem-solving. Whereas women like to rely more on emotional cues and to network in their approach. How often do we hear a complaint from a man? 'We have discussed all this before, so there is no need to go over it again', suggesting that the problem is resolved. The woman, on the other hand, does not feel right and needs to talk further. There is no easy answer to this situation, and many couples have to find a way to compromise or agree to differ.

## Interpretations

In relationships, it may be that you think someone does not care because of their actions. Doubt creeps in, and we can make assumptions like, 'They don't like me'. This can happen in both sexes, although it does appear to be more prevalent with women. This could be because men appear to find it easier to compartmentalise their thoughts. Generally, men are good at being in the 'work mode' and then in 'leisure mode', whereas women generally merge the different aspects of their lives. This is not intended to be a sexist comment; generally, women are just more likely to think about several things simultaneously, whereas men tend not to do that as much. For example, men are less likely to think about their relationship while at work. This can come as a surprise to a woman when they ask if their man has thought about an unresolved issue during the day and the man replies, 'Haven't given it any thought'. This can be misinterpreted as they do not care, but that is probably not the reality.

People are not mind readers. We need to remember to think about how clearly, we communicate. When it is left to chance, problems can arise.

"We are often afraid of being responsible for someone else's happiness"

Another difficulty can be that men will often report that they can never seem to do enough for their partner. There is a desire for us all to make each other happy, although as we have established, this needs to come from within. Having the responsibility of 'making' someone else happy can play very heavy on a relationship.

## Model of a relationship

We have looked at the power of values in life and how they influence so many of our decisions, hopes and dreams. We have also said that having a shared understanding of these values can strengthen a relationship.

When we are thinking about our values, including our hopes and dreams, we need to ensure that this is explicit. When we understand what the relationship model will be like or feel like for ourselves, then we can communicate this to our partner. We so often are not clear or sure what we are looking for or wanting, so no wonder it is difficult to find.

Once we have established this for ourselves, then we need to communicate it. The power comes from also hearing their values and then gaining an understanding of their interpretation. This helps to bring your interpretations closer and reduce doubt. For example, we often have a difference in how to love and be loved. People express love in different ways. Just because love is expressed a certain way does not mean anyone's love is stronger than another's. It may just mean love is shown in different ways. Therefore, how one person interprets love to another may be different. This is true for all parts of the relationship, not just love. It is important to understand other key values like trust, honesty, even romance, and the components of the relationship. When we establish these understandings, we can enhance our connection.

The risk of not doing this can lead to the possibility of misinterpretation, which can lead to frustration, disappointment and ultimately resentment.

## Love languages

Gary Chapman, an author, pastor and speaker, introduced the concept of love languages in his 1992 bestseller, *The 5 Love Languages*. He suggested that people prefer to receive love in one of five ways: words of affirmation, quality time, acts of service, physical touch or receiving gifts.

In relationships, people tend to express love to a partner in the way they would personally most like to receive it. It is important to identify what your love language is first so that you can communicate with your partner. Otherwise, there is a risk that your or your partner's efforts are unappreciated. For example, you might make a gorgeous meal and hope that your partner is happy, but you made a bit of a mess in the kitchen and they flipped out at that. They may prefer to come home to a tidy house than a meal, so your efforts are not seen positively.

It is important to identify what your love language is first so that you can communicate with your partner. Otherwise, there is a risk that your or your partner's efforts are unappreciated. For example, you might make a gorgeous meal and hope that your partner is happy, but you made a bit of a mess in the kitchen and they flipped out at that.

They may prefer to come home to a tidy house than a meal, so your efforts are not seen positively.

## Needs

It sounds obvious that we would communicate our needs to our partner, and yet this can be less common. We are often frustrated with our partners before we have been honest with ourselves. Have we been clear about what is important and why? The other person may be completely unaware of the impact.

We then stay in drama when we do not speak up and then feel upset. This plays out for both parties and the discord between each becomes the bigger problem.

When a relationship is not working for either party, it is vital to talk. Problems can often arise from a difference of understanding. Things can be worked out and a plan made so that both needs are being met. If not, do not be afraid to look for a partner who can give you the love you deserve.

We are coming to the end of our journey together – making sense of relationships. Spending some time looking at some of the differences around communication styles is useful although please be aware this is a huge topic and basically everything in this book and *A Path Travelled – How to make sense of your life* – is all about communication. The final chapter is a mini reminder of what is really critical to have the relationship you want.

# CHAPTER EIGHT

# The Right Place

## People can change

We need to want to make changes, and we need to be able to identify what we want to change first. The old adage "A leopard can't change his spots" is often linked to "People cannot change". We know that this is not true, and we also know that people sometimes change too much.

However, people *can* change.

What they are unable to do, though, is just snap their fingers and say goodbye to well-established patterns, even when those patterns result in bad consequences. We do not change 'just' because someone (even ourselves) wants us to.

However, the opposite stance is also filled with flaws. Chase away those demons that tell you that you cannot change, it is too hard, it is in your DNA or requires excessive effort. Such a mindset will sabotage your efforts before you even begin. Though it is true that 'you are who you are' and that your personality structure 'is what it is', it is not true that you cannot modify, alter, or tweak many aspects of how you behave.

So, how do you change?

It is a process that begins with being aware. This may seem obvious, but it is not. If you are used to blaming everyone else for your problems, then you are not aware. If you are living your life in a daze, blaming it on bad luck, then you are in denial. How will you ever change anything if you do not own up to how you are thinking and that your behaviour is helping create the predicament you are in?

" Don't let the speed bumps in life become 'stop signs... "

Self-awareness without judgement is the first step. You can, however, be fully aware of your bad habits and still not change. A no-nonsense commitment to change is needed. A casual commitment will not do. Going on a diet for a week does not hack it!

What is a no-nonsense commitment to change? In your quiet moment of truth, when you are alone and not under pressure by anything or anyone, you, your 'true' self, in harmony with your 'emotional' self, make a solemn pledge to change.

You acknowledge the need for self-discipline, perseverance and hard work. You know why you want to change. You know who you want to be. You know that your actions need to adhere to your beliefs. You know it makes no sense claiming you want to change but then do nothing about it. You are tired of disappointing yourself. You are fed up with feeling frustrated. You are drained from not being yourself and having the life you deserve.

Adopting new ways rarely comes comfortably at first. You may feel a lot of resistance to change. But if you think about change as an opportunity to grow, not as an unwanted burden, amazing things can happen.

Muhammad Ali said, "A man who views the world the same at fifty as he did at twenty has wasted thirty years of his life."

Even moderate change can reap meaningful benefits. Change that moves in a positive direction will not only expand your confidence but can also empower your well-being and enrich your relationships.

In this chapter, we will summarise the key principles that we have explored throughout the book.

## Remember it all starts with yourself

The most important relationship we will ever have is with ourselves. We often spend a lot of time and energy trying to make relationships work, and in this pursuit, we neglect the relationship with ourselves.

Each relationship can get us nearer and nearer to being our true self, and in the end, the best version of us emerges. When we are able to show up in a relationship, we have usually made it in both ways. We are being ourselves and we have found a partner who is able to see you as that person.

When we have explored our inner-self and found emotional freedom from our own inner demons, we are then ready to have a healthy relationship with someone. Or we can work on this while in a relationship, although we need to be mindful of the emotional responses which come as self-protection. These responses are a signal that there is inner discord or tension.

It is important to work towards knowing that you deserve to have good things in your life and support the notion that you also deserve a good relationship. When you have self-belief and self-worth, you will make the right changes and therefore attract a good partner.

Relationships are an external view of both party's inner world. The better you treat yourself and believe in yourself, the healthier a relationship can be.

Feeling happy, content, and secure about yourself in a relationship is how you know you are onto a good thing.

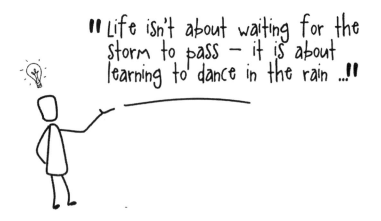

"Life isn't about waiting for the storm to pass – it is about learning to dance in the rain ...!"

It is really important to think about what you need to do to help yourself, whether in or out of a relationship. Taking some time to think about what is in your checklist for looking after yourself is key to identifying how you will tackle any challenges.

Take some time to look at this for yourself with the next exercise.

# STEP to CHANGE

## Looking After Yourself

# Looking after yourself

Checklist for looking after yourself

- take time each day for yourself

- check your perspective and responses

- give yourself time and space to reflect and be alone

- learn something new

- be kind to yourself

- be playful and keep things light

- reach out to others

What will you be doing for each of these areas?

## Nothing is perfect

Most of our relationships have parts that are great and parts that can be challenging. The main point is to be able to notice if, or what part we play, and what we can learn.

A successful couple feels that they are happier for having their partner in their life. Each party does not want to change the other. 'When you listen to your heart, you'll feel whether or not the person you're dating is right for you'. When you feel good, feel that your partner is patient and true, treats you the same in public as he/she does at home, then you are on the right path.

A healthy relationship will enhance your life, but it is vital to check that you are not relying on it to fulfil it completely. This will lead to pressure and expectations, which are likely to lead to disappointment.

## Checklist for a healthy relationship

As with the task of looking at what you need to do in your checklist for a healthy you, it is important to be honest about what you want or have got in your relationship or situation.

You could, on the one hand, be choosing to be single and are happy with this, ensuring that there are no negative traits like guilt or anger around which are holding you back.

Wherever you are, in terms of a relationship, it is vital to be courageous, vulnerable and honest with yourself to ensure you get what you deserve and a relationship where you can grow and develop as a person.

# STEP to CHANGE

Your Healthy Relationship

## Your Healthy Relationship

Key components, which are certainly not set in stone to a healthy relationship, can be measured in terms of the following:. Take some time to think about this for yourself.

Contentment: - how much of the day/time do you feel content?

Effortless – are you putting in a lot of work or managing a lot of negativity?

Equality – does the relationship offer give and take? Do you both have a voice? Do you have choices?

Values and language — are they similar, or do you have an understanding of the differences?

Expectations — are you on the same page?

Bounce back — how quickly do you recover from a difficult time?

Resilience — can you rely on each other and offer support?

## Are you really ready?

We need to watch out for the need or desire to be in a relationship. As we have explored, we can be desperate to meet the right person, yet we were not 'really' ready. We have our own limits, doubts, confusion and do not love and respect ourselves.

The take-home message from this book is to be truly focused on yourself and what you can learn about yourself in relationships. These can turn out to be personal gems.

## About Alison Blackler

Alison is a coach, facilitator and Author. This is her second book in the 'Path Travelled' series.

Alison is most interested in us all understanding ourselves and then learning how to communicate with each other better. She takes this message through her 1:1 client sessions, her work with leaders and in businesses, prisons and schools.

She has made her own personal journey part of both books. She describes every experience as teaching us something valuable and has a desire to fast-track others into this thinking.

Her passion is people, and she feels so lucky to love her work.

Being a people person, Alison's family and friends are hugely important to her. She has a love of life, being outside and active and will have a go at most things!

Alison is based in the Northwest and shares her home with her boyfriend Danny and her many pets!

# A SPECIAL THANK YOU

As ever I am always grateful to my wonderful friends, family, colleagues and clients. Without realising you all inspire me and keep me focused and motivated. I want to honour two special friends who sadly both passed away the week this book was finished. They are both strong, beautiful inspiring shining lights – Wendy Baker and Kelly Morrison.

Writing this book has been a completely different experience than the first although I am still indebted to everyone who has been involved.

To the wonderful Annie Lawrenson again for the typesetting, the illustrations and for her ongoing patience and friendship. Both my books have been as much hers as mine.

To Sue Miller and Estelle Maher from Team Author UK for getting the book edited and published.

To Emily Smith and Arlisa Gilronan for reading through the manuscript and giving valuable feedback, like 'I don't know what you mean here'.

To Daniel Moore for his ongoing support and love. And for listening to me reading the whole book out loud in its earliest form.

To Ross Makepeace for his creativity and design of the book cover.

To Daniel Dawson for taking my profile picture.

## Share with us

I hope you have enjoyed your journey with me. It is my intention to have inspired you to take some steps forward in your life and relationships, knowing that you can and that you have choices. I would love to hear your thoughts, reflections and exciting life changes after reading this book.

Visit my website **www.2-minds.co.uk**, sign up to my newsletter and please do leave a review.

Visit my Facebook page
**www.facebook.com/2minds**

Connect with me on Instagram
**www.instagram.com/alison2minds**

I am available for public speaking and would be delighted to chat about possible events.

Wishing you all the success, happiness and love in your life,

*Alisa*

Printed in Great Britain
by Amazon